THE MILITARY MILLIONAIRE

THE MILITARY MILLIONAIRE

CRAIG D MORROW

C M
Education

CONTENTS

First Printing, 2025

CHAPTER 1

Introduction

If you are one of the small number of Americans who qualify for service in the armed forces, you have a pathway to lifetime wealth and financial independence available to you. This book will show you that path. The financial pathway laid out here provides details of the actions you will take at every step of your military career. The example career pathway has you retiring at 24 years of service with over $1,000,000 in your retirement account and a total retirement income at the age of 59 ½ of almost $100,000 a year – for life! That is financial independence. No job, no hassle, and still earning $100,000 a year. . . and all long before you're old enough to claim Social Security (which will provide even more income!).

This plan is not about living under a bridge and eating nothing but peanut butter sandwiches for twenty years. If you follow this plan, **you will be able to spend as much money as the average American of your age**. This plan acknowledges that you will likely get married, and you will likely have children. These are great things that enhance your quality of life, but they have a financial cost; this plan understands these are necessary costs and therefore incorporates these realities. This book will show you how a career in the United States military can allow you to **enjoy life AND build substantial wealth**. This book is also not about how to "Get Rich Quick." You will notice words like "long-term" in this book; you will not be told that it is "quick." There is no reliable way to get rich quick. Yes, you might win the lottery; you might buy the right stock at the right time, but these involve luck. This plan does not rely upon you getting lucky. This book will show you how –by committing to developing lasting wealth– you can secure a life free from financial worries. The plan presented in this book identifies 16 key moments during a 24-year military career when you need to take specific actions to achieve the dual goals of maintaining a standard of living on par with the average civilian of your same age while also growing the substantial wealth that will provide you with financial freedom after your military career concludes.

Any service member who follows this plan can achieve "financial independence." Financial independence means being able to do what you want to do, not what your boss says you must do. This does not simply mean you are your own boss – ask any business owner, the business is their boss; it tells them what they must do and when they must do it. Financial independence means, quite simply, that if you don't want to get out of bed at a certain time, you don't have to – and you'll still be able to feed your family.

Financial independence does not mean that you can fly your family and friends to Paris for lunch every Thursday ("spend money"). This plan will show you how to become a millionaire, and being a millionaire allows you to enjoy life; it does not allow you to waste money. That's a fast track to poverty for almost anyone. It doesn't matter if you are a surgeon, an NFL quarterback, or an Oscar-winning actor. If someone makes ten million dollars a year, but spends eleven million, they have no wealth. When their income stream dries up, they will be learning how to get food stamps. You, on the other hand, will slowly but steadily grow wealth while maintaining a lifestyle equivalent to the average American. When you have your million dollars and decide to quit work and spend your time volunteering in the local soup kitchen, you may be serving that former pro athlete. Financial independence means you don't *need* a job (if you *want* a job, you can choose to do something you enjoy). Financial independence means you are not reliant upon an employer to put a roof over your head and meals on the table. Financial independence means you don't have to worry about money, ever.

To enjoy life – actually, just to get through life – you need one of two things:

1) a job that provides you with an income, or
2) a pile of money that generates an income.

Most people understand these very simple concepts. If I work at Mr. Hooper's store, he will reward my effort with money (I have a job). If I take that money and put it in the bank, they will pay me interest just for letting them use that money. My small pile of money is earning money for me (although very little). The bank is willing to pay me interest because they can use my money as part of a much bigger pile of money that makes the bank much more money. This book will help you create a much bigger pile of money.

When we are young, none of us (with rare exceptions) has a pile of money that we can use to produce enough income to support us, so we get jobs. When we get older, we ultimately become unable to work. Even if you keep your health, you are likely to reach a point in life where you'd rather spend your time *not* working at a job. A big pile of money is the answer. A pile of money, well-invested, just silently generates more money for you. . . day after day, year after year. Unlike rental real estate, a pile of money isn't going to create calls in the middle of the night. This book shows you the path to that creating that big pile of money. It is that big pile of money that will provide you with your financial independence.

As you read this book, you need to always keep one thought in mind: data matters. Everything presented in this book is based on real-world data, not stories that your Uncle Dave told you. All of us have probably had friends, family members and co-workers talk about most of the topics in this book. There is a fair chance that what they told us was wrong. They certainly believed everything they said but, like much of what we hear, it was probably based on opinion, rumor, and/or "common sense." None of these are inherently reliable or factual. When reading this book, you will see every fact is supported with a reference citation, providing a reliable source for all the information. You need to trust the data more than "Uncle Dave."

A second thing to keep in mind is that this book uses real numbers. It uses the actual military pay rates and the actual incomes and expenses for Americans of various ages and family compositions. The numbers are used to determine the percentages, but it is the percentages that you need to focus on. Those numbers will change over time (most likely getting bigger due to inflation). However, this book provides guidance to you in terms of percentages of your pay to invest. These percentages are enduring. Regardless of the year or what actual dollar figure military pay may have grown to by some year in the future, if you use the percentages provided here, you will achieve the goal.

Understanding Retirement

Let me begin by saying "Yes, you do need to think about retirement now." Sometime after everyone begins their working life, they begin to think about retirement. Sometimes this is because of prudent foresight; sometimes this is because of something that happened at work that prompts a "take this job and shove it" stream of thought. Whatever may prompt you to begin thinking about retirement, it is indeed worthy of genuine thought and planning; sooner is much better than letter.

What is Retirement? Retirement is, quite simply, the phase of your life that comes after you stop working. Retirement is also a relatively new idea. Before about 1900, most men –at that time it was typically men whose labor provided the principal financial support for the family– continued their professional labors until they died.[1] In pre-industrial America, the typical family earned their income from agriculture or artisanal enterprises. When the patriarch became unable to perform the physical labors their work required, they tended to move into a role of supervising younger family members and/or hired employees.

In the middle of the 19th Century, some government employees (e.g., police and firefighters) began to receive pensions from their employers. In 1875, the American Express Company began to offer a pension to its employees. [2] From these beginnings sprang the idea of spending our twilight years in a period of relative ease. As life-expectancy has increased, the American conception of retirement has morphed from a few years of relative ease to a period of a decade or more spent on the golf course or engaged in other leisurely pursuits.

The reality is that most of us seek to spend a substantial portion of our adult lives doing what we want to do, rather than what our employer wants us to do. And this is indeed possible, but it takes planning, it takes sacrifice, and it takes time. The retirement you likely envision will not "just happen." **Without deliberate action on your part, you are likely to have a much lower standard of living in retirement than you enjoyed during your working years**; this does not need to be the case.

What about Social Security? Let's begin this discussion with some history of the Social Security program. When the Social Security program was implemented in 1935, the average life expectancy for an American man was just over 60 years old. [3] Social Security, however, did not payout any old-age benefits until the recipient reached the age of 65.[4] It is too simplistic to say that the average person would therefore never collect old-age benefits from Social Security. The reality is that infant (and juvenile) mortality in the United States was still relatively high in the early twentieth century; this makes overall life expectancy lower than the life expectancy for an adult. Nonetheless, of the men who made it to the age of 21, fewer than 54% would live to collect Social Security at the age of 65.[5] Although, the law directed that an amount was to be collected from everyone's paycheck (3% in 1948), only about half of the people who had paid into the program ever received *any* retirement benefit.[6] That's obviously not good news for the people who were required to pay into a program they never benefited from, but it should be good news for you. The fact that the Social Security program was getting more money in taxes than it paid out in benefits allowed the Social Security Trust Fund to grow fairly quickly. In 1942, the first year the Social Security Act of 1935 allowed for the payment of federal old-age benefits, the government collected just over $1 billion from the new Social Security tax and paid out a little less than $166 million in federal old-age benefits. The net effect of the Social Security tax was the addition of $926 million to the federal revenues. The next year (1943), the surplus payments to the government exceeded $1 billion; this new tax continued to add more than $1 billion a year to the federal government coffers until 1955.[7]

However, as life expectancies have increased, the Social Security Trust Fund has been stressed. A recent study estimated that a woman turning 65 in 2060 would receive $422,000 in Social Security benefits in retirement but would have only paid $257,000 into the program.[8] Although this example is for a low-income earner (Social Security provides proportionally greater benefits for low earners compared to high earners), it remains true that the Social Security program as it exists in 2025 is not sustainable. As of May 2024, the Social Security Administration expects the Trust Fund to be depleted by the year 2035, and that's probably before you expect to retire. The bottom line here is that you cannot expect Social Security to be around –or at least not a generous as it is today– when you do retire.

In November of 2024, the average Social Security payment to a retiree was just $1,925.46.[9] That works out to a little over $23,000 a year. This is less than the starting salary in the military (for someone who has all their meals and housing provided!). It is also not far from poverty. In 2024, a person making up to $19,587 qualifies for food stamps; the average Social Security payment is only about $68 a week above the income level that qualifies someone to receive food stamps. Is this the retirement you dreamed of? Social Security is a good idea, but it pays out more than it takes in; this is unsustainable. Social Security benefits are good to have –any money is good to have– but they are not sufficient to provide a comfortable retirement. At best, Social Security will provide a supplement to your retirement; it cannot be your retirement.

What about my pension? As was mentioned earlier, pensions began to be offered by employers in the later 19th Century. In the beginning, most pensions were "defined benefit" pensions. A "defined benefit" retirement plan tells you exactly what your benefit will be when you retire (your benefit is defined in advance). Typically, this involved the employer promising to pay the retired employee some percentage of the previous salary every month until the employee died. However, a simple example can illustrate the financial burden that defined benefit pensions place on a business. Consider an employer that pays their employees $100,000 a year in salary and provides a defined benefit pension equal to 50% of the employee's salary after 30 years of service. After 30 years of service, a 50-year old retiree would receive half their salary for the rest of their life (about another 30 years). Ignoring inflation, this means that the employer must pay $3 million in salary while the employee is working and another $1.5 million in retirement benefits. In effect, the employer is getting 30 years of labor at a cost of $4.5 million (or $150,000 a year). As people began to live longer and longer, the financial burden of these pensions became too much for many companies to bear and they either filed for bankruptcy to get out from under these burdens (Delta Airlines, United Airlines, etc.) or simply ceased operations (Trans World Airlines, Bethlehem Steel, etc.). A defined benefit pension is a substantial expense for the employer.

Now consider the "defined contribution" pension plan. A defined contribution plan tells you exactly what the employer will contribute to your retirement savings while you are working (their contribution is defined), rather than what you will be paid in retirement. If the employer in the example above converts to a defined contribution pension, offering a 5% contribution to the employee's retirement plan (e.g., 401K plan), their total cost for a year of the employee's service would be $105,000, rather than the $150,000 cost for the defined benefit plan described above. For this reason, almost all employees (other than government employees) are now offered a defined contribution pension, rather than a defined benefit pension. In 2025, if your company offers a pension at all, it is almost certainly a defined contribution plan. A defined contribution pension plan is a nice thing, but it requires you to contribute funds, and manage the investment of those funds (or pay someone else to do so).

The military has also taken a step away from a retirement that is exclusively a defined benefit plan. Since 2018, the U.S. military has provided a blended retirement system (BRS). This combines a defined benefit pension and a defined contribution pension. This will be covered in more depth later in this book. At this point, the important thing to consider is that almost all civilian employers have stopped offering defined benefit pensions, but the military continues to do so (although less generous than the pre-2018 pension).

A second thing to consider is that the typical military pension –as generous as it is– only replaces a portion of your active-duty income. As an example, at the end of a twenty five-year military career, a good military leader will have likely been promoted six times, to the rank of Sergeant First Class (Army), Gunnery Sergeant (Marine Corps), Chief Petty Officer (Navy) or Master Sergeant (Air Force). In the final years of their active-duty career, this person will make approximately $6357 a month in "base pay," a tax-free subsistence allowance of $466 and a tax-free allowance of $1,953 to house their family in central Texas for a total monthly income (after taxes) of $8,813. In retirement, their defined benefit pension (after 25 years of service) will provide a monthly income, after taxes, of about $3,110. That is only about 37% of their preretirement income; this leaves you with two choices: 1) do not retire and get a post-military job, or 2) live a much more modest life in retirement. The defined benefit military pension is a great thing, but it is insufficient to provide a comfortable retirement by itself.

CHAPTER 2

Understanding Military and Non-military Income

How much money does the "average" American make? The answer to this question is at the very heart of the model presented in this book. It is vital that you understand just what the truth is. The lifestyles typically represented on television are, unsurprisingly, not reflective of reality. No one believes that rich and famous we see on television have the same standard of living that the average American does. We aspire to that level of riches, but we understand they are not like most of us. Unfortunately, we are also misled when we "ordinary" people portrayed in the media. The young woman living in an expansive New York City apartment, while working as a barista or as a writer at a fashion magazine, is not reality. The average barista in New York City makes about $17 per hour, or a little more than $35,000 a year.[10] The average fashion writer in New York City makes a little more than $26 an hour (just over $55,000 a year).[11] Contrast this income with the cost of rent in New York City, where the average rent is more than $87 per square foot.[12] After taxes (Federal income tax, Medicare, Social Security, state income tax, NYC income tax), our fashion writer is left with about $3,050 each month. If she spends 100% of her income on rent, she could rent a 34-square-foot apartment (less than 6 foot square). Not big enough to fit a twin bed (the mattress alone is 75 inches long), and certainly nothing like television would lead us to believe. Indeed, if our fashion writer budgets her money effectively (allowing her to eat, bath, and do other things we all enjoy), she would spend about 25% of her gross income on housing. That brings the money available for rent down to about $1,145 each month. This is enough to rent about 13 square feet in New York (about enough space to sit down). Clearly, what we see in the media is typically very different from reality.

Unfortunately, we cannot rely on what we see in real life either. As you will read again later in this book, most Americans fall into one of two groups: 1) people who *spend* money people, and 2) who *have* money. Most American fall into the first group. A recent study found that 41 percent of "Gen Z" (born between 1995 and 2010) have a *negative* net worth![13] That's right, your neighbor owes money more than she has in the bank. One way to think of this: If you have no debt, and you have $1 in your pocket, you might be in the top half of your generation in terms of wealth. Your friends may have nicer cars and nicer apartments that you, but you can reasonably assume they have no wealth; they are spending every penny they have, and then spending more! Their lifestyle might be nicer than your today, but this behavior is not sustainable. More on that later.

To get the answer to the question of how much our peers are actually making, we turn to the data collected by the United States government. Using data collected by the Bureau of Labor Statistics, we find that Americans between the ages of 20 and 24 earn an average of $784 a week. The median weekly earnings for people between the ages of 25 and 34 was $1,136. People aged 35 to 44 earned an average of $1,356. Between the ages of 45 and 54, the usual weekly earnings were $1,336. Earnings continue to drop from this point.[14] It is worth noting that these averages are for the entire population. If we look at Americans who graduated high school, but did not go to college we find the average weekly pay for high school graduates over the age of 25 is $930 a week. Americans with some college or an associate's degree earn an average of $1,056 each week.[15] This is still below the overall average; the overall average (the higher number) is the measure we will use in this book when we look at civilian income. What this means is that we will be comparing your military compensation to a group with an average income *higher* than Americans with an associate's degree. Additionally, although the median earnings for Americans begins to go down after turning 45, the model used in this book will assume your peers have remained healthy and fully employed. Therefore, we will assume that your peers continue to earn at the higher rate of the 35- to 44-year-old group ($5,876 a month), rather than the lower earnings of the 45- to 54-year-old group ($5,876 a month). The chart below provides the truth about what your peers are earning; later in the book, we will look at what they are spending.

Age	Median Earnings	Monthly Income
20- to 24-years old	$40,768/year ($784/week[16])	$3,397
25- to 34-years old	$59,072/year ($1,136/week[17])	$4,923
25- to 34-years old (2-person household)	$117,296/year[18]	$9,774.67
25- to 34-years old (3-person household)	$100,612/year[19]	$8,384.33
25- to 34-years old (4-person household)	$100,063/year[20]	$8,338.58
35- to 44-years old (4-person household)	$149,755/year[21]	$12,479.58

The chart includes a "Monthly Income" figure to allow us to compare directly with monthly military compensation. The monthly income shown here is simply the weekly earning, multiplied by the number of weeks in a year (52) to provide an annual income, then dividing that by the number of months in a year (12) to get an average monthly income for each age group (or when the government provides annual income, that is simply divided by 12).

Understanding Military Compensation.

Most people don't understand military compensation. That's understandable, given that very few Americans have ever served in uniform; however, even many of the people who have served don't fully appreciate the full scope (and value) of their military compensation. You've probably noticed that I'm referring to military "compensation" and not "pay." As a member of the military, you will of course earn pay (indeed, *good* pay) but you will also receive some very valuable allowances as another part of your total compensation. But even your "pay and allowances" do not represent your full compensation. The following pages describe military compensation more completely.

Understanding Military Rank and Pay Grades.

In any career, your position in the organization is closely related to your income. As you are entrusted with greater responsibilities you will typically be provided with increased pay. In the military, this is reflected by your rank. As your rank (and responsibilities) increase, your pay will increase. The amount of responsibility you are entrusted with is intimately related to your military rank, and your military rank is intimately related to your military income.

Greater Rank => Greater Responsibility => Greater Income.

Because of this, it is worthwhile to take a moment to discuss the rank (and pay) structure of the military in a little more depth. Many people in the military use the terms "rank" and "pay grade" interchangeably. Although the two are closely linked, they are distinct. All "staff sergeants" in the Army and Marine Corps serve in the pay grade of E-6, but not all E-6s are staff sergeants. An E-6 in the Navy or Coast Guard is a "Petty Officer First Class" and an E-6 in the Air Force or the Space Force is a "Technical Sergeant."

Similarly, two Soldiers can serve the Army in the pay grade of E-4, but one could hold the rank of "Specialist" and the other could be a "Corporal." These two servicemembers are the same pay grade, in the same service, but different ranks. A corporal is senior to ("outranks") a specialist, even though they serve in the same pay grade. In the Army, a Soldier can also serve in the paygrade of E-8 as either a "Master Sergeant" or a "First Sergeant." In the Air Force, an airman can serve in the rank of "First Sergeant" as an E-7, E-8 or E-9.

Given the financial focus of this book, we will focus on your career progression through the various pay grades, rather than your progression through the various ranks. This creates commonality across all branches of service; an E-1 in the Army makes exactly the same pay as an E-1 in the Navy, or the Marine Corps, or the Air Force, or the Space Force, or the Coast Guard.

Your Salary ("Basic Pay"). So how much money will I make? It's too early in our conversation to talk actual dollar figures (trust me, that will come), but the biggest part of your compensation will come from your basic pay (or "base pay"). As noted earlier, your pay is directly linked to your military rank. In considering your career in the military, you must understand that no two careers are the same. This is, of course, true whether you are military or a civilian. People are promoted at different times within the same branch of the military and certainly between the different branches, but we can look at the average times for promotion.

Your first promotions in the military will come fairly quickly. With rare exceptions, a high-school graduate enlisting at the lowest pay grade (E-1) would only stay in that pay grade for six months (some will be promoted before six months; the Navy does not promote until nine months of service). After promotion to the second pay grade (E-2), the average service member would spend another six to nine months in that pay grade before being promoted again (and some will, again, be promoted even earlier). During your third year of service, you can expect to get your third promotion (to E-4).

After you have achieved the pay grade of E-4, your promotions will be much less "automatic," and the timelines will begin to vary a lot more. Exceptional performers will be promoted more quickly, and lower performers will be promoted much slower. Let's look at the average times for promotion to E-5 in each of the services: In the Navy, you can expect to become a petty officer 2nd class in about 3.6 years. The Army seeks to promote soldiers to the rank of sergeant at about 4.5 years of service.[22] Marines are promoted to sergeant after about 4.8 years.[23] Finally, in the Air Force, you should expect to wait until you have seven (7) years of service to pin on staff sergeant.[24]

For the example career timeline used in this book, a rough average across the services is used. This is a realistic timeline but, some of you will progress more slowly and many of you may progress even faster. In any case, the faster you can get promoted, the better your financial situation will be, not just immediately, but in the long-term as well.

If you spend a career in the military, and do your job well, you can reasonably expect to earn promotion to the pay grade of E-7 (Sergeant First Class in the Army, Chief Petty Officer in the Navy and Coast Guard, Gunnery Sergeant in the Marine Corps, or Master Sergeant in the Air Force or Space Force). You can aim to rise to the higher ranks (the E-8 and E-9 pay grades), but know that the women and men who earn these ranks are exceptional; the overwhelming majority of servicemembers will never reach these levels.

In 2025, the lowest basic pay rate (for an E-1 with less than four months of service) is $1,949.10 a month. This is a respectable salary, but it is only part of your total compensation. Indeed, for the four months that you are paid at this rate, it is almost certain that your housing and meals will be provided at no cost; making all of your basic pay "disposable income" that you can spend on anything your choose (which should, of course, include investing for retirement).

If you stay in for a 30-year career and reach the highest ranks, your basic pay as an E-9 after 30 years of service would be $9,374 a month ($112,489 a year); as impressive as this figure is, it is still only part of your total military compensation. Do well professionally and you will do well financially.

The Big Picture.

So, what's it all worth? Let's imagine, you have just finished your training (usually about six months or so in duration) and are now an E-2 stationed at Fort Cavazos, Texas (an area with a cost of living that is about 80% of the national average).[25] Your basic pay for 2025 would $31,190. You will likely be living in the barracks, but if you were living off base your housing allowance would equal $15,588 for the year. It is also likely that you would be getting all of your meals for free; if not, you would receive an annual Basic Allowance for Subsistence (BAS) totaling $5,589.24. The tax advantage you enjoy –because you don't need to pay income tax on your housing allowance or your BAS– is equal to $2,117.70. The estimated value of your medical coverage is at least **$5,488 (for you as a single person)**. So, at the very start of your career, your compensation package is worth almost $60,000 a year! Compare that with the average personal income in this area of $24,941.[26] You're less than a year out of high school and making more than twice as much as the people around you, not to mention the fact that you are also earning a pension and get four weeks of paid vacation every year. In the later years of your career, you would be earning much more; in fact, 20 years into your career you would be making more than twice as much as you made at the start. The total compensation for an E-7, with a spouse and kids, living in the Fort Cavazos area would be well over $100,000 –four times what your "average American" neighbor is bringing home.

Annual Pay Increases and Allowances. Every year, based on Congress approving it, the military gets a pay increase. This is intended to keep your purchasing power the same. Prices increase because of inflation, so your pay need to increase as well. If prices are going up a lot, you'll get a big pay increase in January. If prices are basically staying the same, you will get a smaller increase (or possible no increase at all). This money is intended to offset inflation. If you spent $100 on haircuts last year, then get a 3% annual pay increase in January, you'll probably find that you need to spend $103 on haircuts the next year (the cost of living has gone up 3%). This annual adjustment is not a "raise"; it simply allows you to *maintain* your lifestyle.

Allowances

To understand the model set out in this book, there is one area of military compensation that you must understand and appreciate: Allowances. Allowances are funds provided to service members to offset specific expenses. If the government is giving you an allowance, it is not "free money," it is intended to pay a specific expense. Fortunately the military provides allowances for housing and food (if they are not providing you with housing and food). If you understand that the average American spends about 30% of their income on housing, you understand that receiving housing from the government (or a housing allowance) is like getting a 30% pay raise. Another nice thing about allowances is that they are not subject to any taxes; you get to keep every dollar of your allowances to pay the expenses they are intended to pay.

Free Housing... or more money: Basic Allowance for Housing (BAH). At the very start of their career, most service members will initially live in government-provided quarters (barracks/dormitories). That is, they will be **given a place to live by the military and will not have to pay for this major expense**. The fact that the military provides free room and board to all service members (or a payment for service members to pay for their own meals and/or housing) is an enormous financial benefit and a great advantage over almost any civilian employer.

As they grow in their careers and/or families, service members will eventually move into a home. This home may be provided by the government (on-base housing) or it may be a private home. If the military does not provide you with housing "in kind" –that is, either a room in the barracks or family quarters on post– you will be given money to pay rent for a private home (including utilities!).

But housing costs vary significantly between markets! Housing is San Francisco is going to cost significantly more than the national average of $1221.09; conversely, housing in rural Arkansas is going to be significantly less than the average. Fortunately, Basic Allowance for Housing (BAH) varies by location to account for the different cost of housing in different markets.

Additionally, BAH (unlike the Basic Allowance for Subsistence, or "BAS") is intended to accommodate the whole family, not just the service member. You will, no doubt, hear some service members say "BAH doesn't come close to paying my rent." Could an 18-year-old Soldier choose to rent a 4,000 square foot five-bedroom home? Sure! Will their BAH cover that expense? No. The BAH rates are determined by surveying renters in each local market for their cost of ***rent and utilities***, so most of the people in that area are covering their housing costs for the BAH amount; you should be able to do the same. BAH is not intended to provide luxurious accommodations, but it does provide for your needs. Again, you will be provided government housing, or money to house you and your family. This means if you get married young (that is, in your first few years of service), you will be given a housing allowance that allows you to rent a 1-bedroom apartment. After about three years in the military, you should be promoted to E-5; in this case, you would be paid for an amount that allows you to live in a 2-bedroom townhouse (or duplex). Just a few years after that, when you are promoted to E-6, you would be paid enough to rent a 3-bedroom.

All Your Meals are Free... or you get more money: Basic Allowance for Subsistence (BAS). The service member is either provided meals "in kind," or paid a Basic Allowance for Subsistence (BAS), commonly known as "separate rations." This allowance is intended to feed the service member, so it does not provide additional money to feed any family members you may have. Many service members simply think of this as "food money," and are surprised (upset!) when this money is not included in their paycheck whenever they are provided their meals (such as when they are being fed on a ship, "in the field" on a training exercise, or deployed to combat). Remember, this is money to feed the service member. You can set yourself up for disappointment if you simply think of this as extra money because it can –and will– stop if the military is feeding the service member. If you are ever hospitalized in a military hospital, in addition to providing all of your healthcare at no cost, the military will obviously feed you; this is another circumstance where your BAS will be stopped because you are receiving meals "in kind."

Subsistence (meals "in kind," or a subsistence allowance) is provided to the service member 365 days a year – whether on duty or on leave. If you are taking vacation days ("taking leave"), you probably cannot eat in the mess hall. In this case, if you weren't already being paid BAS, you will now be paid a subsistence allowance while on leave.

Two interesting quirks of subsistence payments arise when you travel wither on Temporary Duty (TDY) or making a Permanent Change of Station (PCS). Whenever you need to serve away from the post/camp/base where you normally live, the government will pay for you to stay in a hotel (if you cannot stay in military facilities); the government will also pay you to eat in restaurants (if you cannot eat in a military facility). The money paid for lodging, meals and incidental expenses is called "*per diem*." Per diem amounts vary by location to account for the fact that meals and hotel rooms in New York City, for example, cost more than meals and hotels in Muskogee, Oklahoma. Regardless of where the military sends you on your TDY, the part of your *per diem* intended to cover "meals and incidentals" is typically fairly generous. You won't be able to eat lobster every day, but you won't need to eat fast food every day either. **This money is paid in addition to your BAS** (so you will still receive your full BAS). Remember: if the military is making you sleep in a tent, you'll probably get less money in your check that month (because they are feeding you and your BAS is stopped), but if they make you sleep in a hotel, you'll get extra money (to pay the higher cost of meals in a restaurant).

If you are moving between duty stations with your family, the government is effectively telling your family members that they need to be on the plane or in the car with you. Because the military is, in essence, telling your family members where to be, the military will pay you additional money to feed your family. While driving to your new location, family members who are 12 and older will receive 75% of the authorized per diem; dependents under the age of 12 receive 50% of the authorized per diem. If you were to change duty stations in 2025, you would be paid an extra $68 per day that you are traveling to pay for meals. Your spouse (and any other family member 12 years or older) would receive $51 per day and family members under 12 would receive $34 per day. So, a family of two parents and a baby would receive an extra $153 ***every day*** while traveling between duty stations. **This money is paid in addition to your BAS**. Again, sleeping in a tent = less money; sleeping in a hotel = extra money.

Other Allowances

Cash Clothing Replacement Allowance. When you enlist in the military, all of your uniforms are provided at no cost. This includes everything you need, from shoes and socks to underwear to hats and everything in between. When you earn rank, the new insignia will be provided to you. When you earn awards, the ribbons for your uniform will also be provided at no cost. The uniforms you receive when you first enter the military should last you for a few years, but at some point, you will need to replace them; to cover this expense the military provides enlisted service members with a clothing allowance. The amount paid will cover the typical cost of replacing uniforms as they wear out. The specific amount varies from service to service and between genders (for example, Marine Corps uniforms cost more than Navy uniforms and women's uniforms cost more than men's uniforms), but is approximately $400 every year. Previously, the clothing allowance was paid out monthly over the course of the year, so service members needed to save this allowance until they needed to replace a uniform item. Because many young service members just considered this extra money every month, they would just spend that $30 or $40; when they need to replace a $200 uniform coat, they didn't have the money. As a result, the military now pays this allowance in a lump sum once a year (on the anniversary of you joining the military). When this lump sum hits your bank account, it's time to make sure your uniforms are up to snuff. Again, this is an allowance; this means it is paid for a specific purpose. It is not a "pay raise," and it is certainly not "free money." You should plan to spend all of your clothing allowance on keeping your uniforms in good condition. NOTE: Commissioned officers must purchase their own uniforms before being commissioned and they do NOT receive a clothing allowance and must pay out of pocket to maintain their uniforms.

Dislocation Allowance. Over the course of your career, you will be asked to mover several times. There are costs associated with moving, and the military covers these for you. The largest expense –moving your personal property from one place to the next– is handled entirely by the military. The next largest expense –moving you (and your family, if you have one)– is also covered by the military. This could be done by providing you with airline tickets or reimbursing you for the cost of driving your car to your new duty station (and any hotel stays that may be required). But there are other, much smaller costs that come with moving as well. This would include the cost of things like having to throw away half a gallon of milk when you leave your old home (and buying a new gallon at the next duty station), or registering your car in new state, or "connection fees' for your utilities, and dozens of other small expenses. The military compensates you for these expenses through a "Dislocation Allowance." Dislocation Allowance varies by rank and number of family members. At the low end, an E-1 with no family members would be paid $1,802.10. Conversely, an E-9 with a family would be paid $3,997.60. Although Dislocation Allowance can be a fairly large payment, it is not "free money" or "extra income." The military is providing you with this money to offset the costs of moving and you will need to use it for that purpose.

Move-In Housing Allowance (MIHA). Related to Dislocation Allowance is the Move-In Housing Allowance. This serves essentially the same purpose as the Dislocation Allowance, but is paid when you move overseas because there may be additional expenses associated with the country where you are being assigned. Because this is intended to offset any country-specific expenses (and is therefore paid in the local currency), the amount obviously varies by location.

Family Separation Allowance. Family Separation Allowance (FSA) is paid anytime the military requires you to be away from your family for *more than* 30 consecutive days. It is paid monthly and equals $250. This is prorated to $8.33/day for periods less than 30 days, but remember it is only paid for periods greater than 30 days. If you are away from home for 29 days, you get $0; if you are away from home for 30 days, you get $250; if you are away from home for 31 days, you get $258.33. This allowance is intended to offset the costs associated with having to live in two places. Small expenses like paying for an extra hour of daycare because the servicemember isn't home to pick up the kids on Wednesdays, sending letters and packages, extra trips to the store because the servicemember can't stop at the store and pick-up a gallon of milk on the way home, et cetera are covered by the Family Separation Allowance. Because servicemembers who are not supporting a family at their permanent duty station while they are away do not have these expenses, they do not receive FSA. Another thing to remember about FSA: it is paid for more than 30 days of separation. What this means is that if you are sent away on January 1st, your paycheck on February 1st will *not* include FSA; when you are paid on March 1st, you will then get paid the FSA for February (the time after you completed 30 days away from home).

Tax Advantages

A dollar that you must give away is not real income. If you had a choice to live in Place A and make $100,000 a year, or live in Place B and make $150,000 a year for doing the same job, which would you choose? Most of you are going to be hesitant to answer because there must be some important factor differentiating Place A from Place B that isn't being disclosed. You are right, the hidden cost that wasn't mentioned is taxes. Working in Place B requires you to pay 24% Federal Income Tax (due in part to your high income), 15% State Income Tax, and 6.5% Local Income Tax. After taxes, your $150,000 income leaves a total of $81,750 in your pocket. Working in Place A, you will only pay 18% Federal Income Tax (because of your lower income tax bracket), and no income tax at the state or local levels; your $100,000 income puts $82,000 in your pocket. The point here is that taxes matter. A dollar that is not taxed is worth a lot more than a dollar that is taxed.

As mentioned previously, military allowances are not subject to income tax. Throughout your career, you will receive housing (or a housing allowance) and meals (or a subsistence allowance). These can be of significant value; the value of these allowances is made even greater by the fact that they are not subject to taxation (at any level). None of the military allowance are taxable (Housing, Subsistence, Family Separation, Clothing, etc.). Think of it this way: If you and your civilian neighbor live in identical houses and pay the same landlord the same amount in rent, your civilian neighbor is actually paying more than you are. You pay $1,000 in rent and the government gives you $1,000 to pay that bill. Your neighbor pays $1,000 in rent, but must earn $1,421.46 to pay that bill, because they need to pay taxes. If we were to assume they are in the 22% tax bracket, you might guess they would need to make

$1,220 to have $1,000 left to pay the rent. That's a reasonable guess, but you must bear in mind that every dollar your civilian neighbor earns is subject not only to income taxes, but to "payroll taxes" as well. These are the taxes that you pay for Medicare and Social Security, and they amount to another 7.65% that must be paid to the government. You also pay these payroll taxes, but only on your "pay," *not on any allowances.* When accounting for payroll taxes as well as income tax, your neighbor must earn $1,421.46 to have $1,000 left after taxes. The $1,421.46 they earned requires them to pay $108.74 (7.65%) in payroll taxes and $312.72 (22%) in income taxes; this leaves exactly $1,000 to pay their rent.

You might be saying "Only rich people are in the 22% income tax bracket!" That's a reasonable assertion. For most of your military career, you will be below the 22% tax bracket. A single person reaches the 22% tax bracket when their taxable income reaches $48,475 (for married couples the threshold is $96,950). With a standard deduction of $15,000 ($30,000 for married couples), a single person earning $63,475 has reached the 22% tax bracket ($126,950 for married couples). The typical person in the military is unlikely to be subject to the 22% tax bracket, because your allowances are not taxable and base pay does not reach the level that would elevate a single person to the 22% tax rate until the pay grade of E-7 (about 15 years into your career), at which point you are likely to be married. Being married, even an E-9 at the end of a 40-year career would not be in the 22% tax bracket. Let's look at our high-earning Sergeant Major (E-9) in detail. His monthly base pay is $10,336.50 each month. His housing allowance is based on location, so let's say he live at West Point, New York; this makes his monthly housing allowance $4,026. His subsistence allowance (food money) is $465.77. His monthly take home pay with all allowance is $14,858.27, or $178,299 a year. Despite the high income, he is still in the 12% tax bracket because his taxable income is only $94,398 (base pay of $10,336.50 12 months = $124,398 - $30,000 standard deduction), so his total federal tax bill is $24,441.21 ($9,516.45 in payroll taxes and $14,927.76 in income taxes), leaving him with $153,855 after taxes. Now consider his civilian neighbor making the same income of $178,299. His taxable income after subtracting the $30,000 standard deduction is $148,299, well within the 22% tax bracket. As a result, his total federal tax bill is $46,265.72 ($13,640 in payroll taxes and $32,626 in income taxes), leaving him with $132,034 after taxes. In this example, both people are paid exactly the same amount, but our service member has almost $22,000 more in his bank account at the end of the year simply because of the tax advantages of military allowances. The example of an E-9 with 40 years of service, living in a relatively high-cost area, is an extreme example but it clearly illustrates the value of having a part of your compensation excluded from taxation.

State Income Taxes. Only six states and the District of Columbia tax military income the same as civilian income; so, in most cases you will be pay less state income tax to the state than your civilian counterparts. In many cases, you will find you owe no state income tax. If your state is one of the nine states that do not tax income (Alaska, Florida, Nevada, New Hampshire, South Dakota, Tennessee, Texas, Washington and Wyoming), then your military pay is obviously exempt from taxation as well. However, some states that do tax the income of their residents exclude military pay from income tax. These states are: Arizona, Arkansas, Illinois, Iowa, Kentucky, Michigan, Minnesota, Missouri, Montana, New Mexico and Oklahoma. Additionally, many states do not require service members to pay state income taxes if they are serving with the military outside of your state of residence (the state where you lived when you joined the military). The states not taxing military income earned out-of-state are: California, Connecticut (if you spent less than 30 days in the state during the year), Idaho, Maine, New York (if you meet the conditions of non-resident eligibility), Ohio, Oregon (if you spent less than 30 days in the state during the year), Pennsylvania and Vermont. Most other states offer some degree of tax reduction for military pay. The only states that fully tax military pay are: Delaware, the District of Columbia, Georgia, Nebraska, Rhode Island and Utah.

Consider the E-9 in New York state from the previous example, if he is from one of the 28 states that will not tax his income, the gap between him and his neighbor becomes even greater. He will owe zero income tax to his state, but his neighbor will owe New York state an additional 6% of his income ($8,898) bringing the total tax benefit for our Sergeant Major to $30,719 each year. The tax advantages of serving in the military represent real money!

It may seem a lifetime away, but its also worth noting that military retirement pay is not taxed in many states. This tax savings could be worth thousands of dollars a year for the rest of your life after you retire from the military.

You may never serve in a combat zone, but if you do, there are some very generous financial benefits. Serving in a war zone obviously entails a special sacrifice on the part of the service member, and their family. The American people (through their elected representatives) have chosen to recognize that sacrifice by excluding all military income earned in a combat zone from federal income tax. This is called the Combat Zone Tax Exclusion (CZTE). The first impact is that you will obviously have more money left "after taxes." Let's assume you are earning a military income (annual base pay) of $50,000; outside of a combat zone, you would have to pay $5,000 in federal income taxes on leaving you with $45,000 to spend that year. If you earned that same income in a combat zone, you pay NO income taxes and have the full $50,000 to spend – the government has effectively given you a $5,000 bonus for spending this year in a combat zone. Returning to the example of our long-serving Sergeant Major at West Point, New York. While serving at West Point, his federal income tax burden was $14,927.76 a year. If he gets deployed to combat zone, he gets to keep nearly $15,000 more of his income due to the income tax exclusion.

You may qualify for the Earned Income Tax Credit (EITC) if you are deployed to a combat zone for most of the year. Because your military income earned while you are in a combat zone is excluded from your "taxable income," your taxable income for this year (or years) is going to be much lower than it would be otherwise (potentially as low as $0). Because this could classify you as "low income" for tax purposes, you could be eligible for the EITC. The EITC is a tax "credit," which means it adds money to you're the amount of your tax refund – even if you paid no income taxes. If your taxable income is low enough, you have the option to claim this credit on your taxes. You also have the option not to claim this credit. Some people may feel that their "true" income is too high for them to get money from the government for being "poor" – even though their taxable income could be almost $0. That's a matter of personal preference but claiming the EITC (if your income is low enough to do so), is entirely above the board and is in no way "cheating on your taxes."

Cheap (or free) Cost of Living. When you are deployed, your personal cost of living drops to essentially zero. Obviously, if you are supporting a family, you will continue to have those expenses, but the service member could live essentially free during their deployment. You will give up your Basic Allowance for Subsistence ("separate rations", but you will be provided all of your meals at no cost. You will also be provided your housing for free; it might be a tent, but it's free. You will NOT give up your Basic Allowance for Housing; the military realizes that you still need to pay rent – even when you are deployed. In many cases, you will have few opportunities to spend money at all. If you do have the opportunity to spend money, it will be on luxuries (e.g., a Whopper from the Burger King trailer, etc.). The only expenses that you might "have to pay" during your deployment include the cost of haircuts –and this assumes no one in your unit brought a pair of clippers– and personal hygiene products (soap, shampoo, toothpaste, menstrual products, etc.), but often all of these arrive in the "To Any Soldier" boxes sent by the American people.

CHAPTER 3

Other Financial Benefits of Military Service

The "Free" Money: Special Pays, Incentive Pays and Bonuses. The money in these categories is truly "extra." Unlike allowances, which are paid to offset a specific cost (like housing and meals), incentive pays and bonuses are paid to encourage service members (or potential service members) to do something. That "something" could be joining the military, which could earn you an enlistment bonus as high as $50,000. It could be jumping out of an airplane, which would earn you an extra $150 every month you are on "jump status." It could be extending your contract with the military (re-enlisting), which could earn you a re-enlistment bonus as high as $95,000.

Because special pay and incentive pay are not associated with an expense, anyone receiving special pay(s) can invest all of this money and still have the same quality of life as your fellow Americans outside the military (and your fellow service members who do not receive the same special pays). This money can (indeed, it should) be added to your investment portfolio. However, because not everyone will receive these, **the plan in this book will assume that no one is receiving any special pay or bonuses**. The one exception to this assumption concerns "Continuation Pay." Continuation Pay is paid to everyone between eight and twelve years of service, who agrees to continue to serve until retirement. Because everyone who serves a full career in the military will receive this pay, we will include this in our model. Each service has the freedom to manage this incentive, within certain limits, so our model takes the middle ground and assumes the Continuation Pay is received after 10 years of service, at the pay grade of E-6 ($4,585.20 monthly base pay times 2.5 = $11,463 in Continuation Pay). When the Continuation Pay incentive is received, using the model career path in this book, the service member's marginal tax rate is 12%, so the after-tax amount available to invest would equal $10,087.44. Currently, all uniformed services (except the Marine Corps) pay Continuation Pay using a 2.5 multiplier; the Marine Corps uses a 5.0 multiplier, so Marines receive twice as much money for their Continuation Pay bonus.

Some of the Special Pays and Incentive Pays include:

- Hazardous Duty Incentive Pay (HDIP). This is paid service members who volunteer to for a designated "hazardous duty." The most common examples of HDIP include "Jump Pay," "Flight Pay," and "Demolition Pay."
- Jump Pay. Service members designated as a parachutist (or undergoing training to become a parachutist) and required to participate in duty involving parachute jumping from an aircraft while in flight receive $150 per month for static line jumps (the standard military parachute jump) and up to $225 per month for military free fall jumps. Doing a minimum of at least one parachute jump every three months is required to continue receiving this pay.
- Flight Pay (crewmembers). This is paid to service members whose duty involves frequent aerial flight as a crew member. Payment ranges from $110 to $250 per month based on the number of years on flight status. Note: this hazardous duty pay is not paid to career aviators (they receive other financial incentives).
- Flight Pay (non-crewmembers). This is paid to service members whose duties involve frequent aerial flights, but who are not a member of the flight crew. Payment is up to $150 per month.

- Demolition Pay. Service members whose primary duty involves the demolition of explosives or disarming or demolishing explosives (such as explosive ordnance disposal personnel assigned to an explosive ordnance disposal billet) are paid up to $150 for each qualifying month.

Less common examples of hazardous duty are listed below. With the exception of diving duty, which pays up to $240 per month, the pay for these duties is typically $150 per month.

- Diving Duty
- Flight Deck Hazardous Duty
- Duty Involving Toxic Fuels and Propellants
- Maritime Visit, Board, Search, and Seizure Duty (Navy only)
- Polar Region Flight Operations Duty
- Weapons of Mass Destruction Civil Support Team
- Hostile Fire Pay. This paid when you are deployed to a hostile fire area. This is currently $225 a month (You get $225 for each month, or part of a month, that you are in the hostile fire area. One day in the hostile fire area = $225; Thirty days in the hostile fire area = $225; Thirty-two days (two months) in the hostile fire area = $450).
- Imminent Danger Pay. This is the same as Hostile Fire Pay in every way, except the area is classified as an "imminent danger area" rather than a "hostile fire area." An area is either an "imminent danger area" *or* "hostile fire area," so you can receive one pay or the other, but never both at the same time.
- Sea Pay. Career Sea Pay is available to members of the Navy, Marine Corps and Army. It starts at $50 per month, going as high as $750 a month ($477 for Soldiers) as your rank and years of sea duty increase.

Bonuses. The military often offers monetary incentives for service members (or prospective recruits) to agree to serve in certain career fields. This could be an enlistment bonus paid to the recent high school graduate who is enlisting for the first time, or the Soldier/Marine/sailor, airman who signs a new contract to extend their service in the military. These bonuses can be quite substantial. The Army is currently offering enlistment bonuses as high as $50,000; the Navy is offering up to $15,000 for some active duty specialties (and up to $20,000 for some reservists), the Air Force is offering as much as $40,000 for enlisting into a special operations career, the Marine Corps is offering new recruits enlistment bonuses up to $15,000 (and as much as $95,000 for some current Marines to reenlist!).

Military Retirement. As noted earlier, the pension is disappearing from the financial landscape of America, but it still exists in the military. The value of a military retirement is quite substantial, potentially millions of dollars of additional income over the course of a lifetime. Since 2018, the U.S. military has provided a blended retirement system (BRS). This combines a defined benefit pension and a defined contribution pension.

The focus of this book is largely on the "defined contribution" part of this system. This is the part where you exercise the most control over the outcome. The defined benefit portion is not affected by investment returns nor by your contributions. The defined benefit portion of your pension will be what it is; you cannot change that. It is safe; the government is guaranteeing they will pay you that amount of money for your years of service. This is a good thing. However, you will have your happiest and most bountiful retirement if you maximize the defined contribution portion of your retirement.

For the defined contribution portion of your retirement, the government will put money equal to 1% of your base pay into your Thrift Savings Program (TSP), regardless of what you do. They will also match your contributions, up to an additional 4% of your base pay.

Currently, the average American aged 65 and older makes about $65,000 a year; less if they are retired.[27] If you are able to accumulate $1 million in the defined contribution portion of your TSP –which you absolutely can by using the method described in this book– and you apply "the 4% rule," you will be able to withdraw $40,000 a year from your TSP and have and continue making those withdrawals for the rest of your life, without depleting that account. If you retire from the military as early as possible, and at the lowest pay grade possible (E6), the defined benefit portion of your retirement plan will provide at least $24,245 a year. You should serve longer and get promoted to the grade of E7. Serving at the paygrade of E7 until you achieve 24 years of service would, in 2025, provide an annual defined benefit of just over $35,500 a year. Combining the defined benefit and defined contribution elements of the pension allows you to have a total retirement income of more than $75,000 a year! You are earning more than 1½ times the national average and you don't have to get out of bed in the morning (and you are probably still under the age of 50!).

Servicemembers Group Life Insurance. The Servicemembers Group Life Insurance (SGLI) program offers you the option to purchase a comprehensive life insurance policy at very affordable rates. As of 2025, the premium for SGLI is 6 cents per $1,000 of coverage purchased; hence, a quarter-million dollars of life insurance will only cost you $15 a month. Compare this to the civilian market where $500,000 of life insurance costs an average of $40 a month.[28] SGLI coverage is available in $50,000 increments, up to a maximum of $500,000 in insurance. Importantly, the rates are not based on age (they won't go up because you have gotten older) and there are no medical exams required (if you are in the military, you can buy the insurance).

You will also have the opportunity to purchase low-cost life insurance for your spouse. Coverage under the Family SGLI program is sold in $10,000 increments, up to a maximum coverage of $100,000. The cost varies by age, beginning at 45 cents per month for $10,000 of coverage.[29]

Unique Investment Opportunities. The federal government offers a special savings opportunity to service members serving in a combat zone. The Savings Deposit Program allows you to deposit up to $10,000 a year into the program, and the government will pay you 10% interest on the money you deposit. Few investments can offer this kind of return on your money – and none of them will guarantee it!

Regardless of the service you join, you will very likely be offered multiple opportunities to live a very low-cost (almost no-cost!) existence. For those individuals inclined to save aggressively for their future, serving in the military can allow you save and invest almost all of your income. An unmarried service member can live in government provided housing (barracks/dormitory) at no cost to them. They can eat in the mess hall at no cost to them. The only expenses that you *must* pay would be for haircuts and personal hygiene products (soap, shampoo, shaving cream, etc.). This could bring you monthly expenses down to the point where you could save and invest all but maybe $100 a month. I'm sure few of you want to live such an austere life, but I know service members who have saved almost 100% of their income for several years. In any case, military service can sometimes force financial restraint upon you. If the Army sends you to live in the woods for a month-long field training exercise, you may have no opportunity to spend *anything* during that month. When you get back home you will find you have two paychecks waiting for you. Similarly, if the Navy sends you on a six-month cruise in the Western Pacific, you will have occasional port calls where you may buy dinner at a restaurant and some jewelry as a souvenir for your mother, but between port calls you'll find you can only buy so many candy bars from the ship's store before your spending drops to zero. Yes, you can try to spend two-weeks' pay at every port call, or spend a month's pay "blowing off steam" after a month in the woods –and some of your colleagues will certainly try– but you will be much better served by taking advantage of these occasions when the military forces you to save your money.

The G.I. Bill. After you have served 90 days on the active duty, you will have earned the benefits of the G.I. Bill, although you must serve 36 months to earn full (100%) G.I. Bill benefits. You can use this to, essentially, pay 100% of the cost of a four-year degree. You can also transfer this benefit to your wife and/or children. For a career service member, transferring this benefit to your family members is probably the most financially prudent decision, because as a service member, you can take advantage of tuition assistance to pay for your education, while you are still serving on active duty. Although most enlisted service members do not take advantage of this benefit, there are some who earn bachelors degrees – and even graduate degrees – using tuition assistance while serving on active duty.

The G.I. Bill pays 100% of the tuition costs for any public university. As of 2025, they will also pay a little more than $28,900 a year for tuition at private universities. They also pay $1,000 per academic year for books and provide a Monthly Housing Allowance (MHA) equal to the housing allowance for a service member in the pay grade of E-5 (with dependents) at the schooling location.

The G.I. Bill is intended to be for veterans. It provides each qualifying veteran, in essence, with four years (36 months) of college with all costs covered. It is our good fortune that we can share this benefit with our families. Because this is a benefit for the veteran, there is no need to provide more than four years of college as part of the G.I. Bill. You may want it to pay for college for all twelve of your kids, but this isn't a benefit designed for your kids, it's a benefit for you –the veteran– that you are allowed to share with your family members if you choose to do so.

To understand just how valuable this benefit is, consider this example: You transfer all 36 months of your G.I. Bill benefits to your daughter. She is accepted to Penn State (Congratulations!), but you are not a resident of Pennsylvania. You notice that the "Out-of-State" tuition is $41,790 a year; that's $167,160 for four years! The first good news is that the law (specifically the Choice Act of 2015) requires schools to charge students using G.I. Bill benefits no more than the "In-State" tuition rate; that's $20,644 for Penn State (so only $82,576 for four years). The G.I. Bill has already saved you over $84,000 before the first tuition check has even been written. The $82,576 for In-State tuition is still a lot of money, but your G.I. Bill will pay 100% of that. Now you need to plan for room and board. The average dormitory room at Penn State costs $4,545 a semester (although there are options as low as $3,027 a semester). Using the average, your daughter's dorm room is going to cost $9,090 a year.[30] Dining on campus with a "meal plan" will cost you another $2,732 a semester (although there are options as lows as $2,100).[31] That's $14,554 for room and board each year. The G.I. Bill will only pay a housing allowance when school is in session (so nothing during summer break, etc.), but it will pay $1,677 a month while she is in school. If we assume she is in school for 9 months of the year, the G.I. Bill will pay a total of $15,093 a year ($1,677 x 9). So, with a top-tier dining plan and an average room, your daughter will still have $539 a year extra (and you could have been as much as $2,016 more every year by opting for a less expensive dorm room). The G.I. Bill also provides the student with a payment of $1,000 a year to buy books! Your daughter is getting a great education, at a great school, and you don't have to pay anything; she's actually putting money in her pocket! If we consider the cost of your neighbor's son–not receiving G.I. Bill benefits–attending the same school. They would pay $167,160 for tuition, $58,216 for room and board and $4,000 for books. That's a total of $229,376 for the same college experience that cost you nothing! So what is your G.I. Bill benefit worth? Let us round numbers and call it a quarter of a million dollars. But you have two children! That's alright. You can allocate half of your G.I. Bill benefit to each of them (or however you want to allocate the 36 months of benefits). They will still get In-State tuition and they'll still get the same benefits for the number of months that you allocated to them.

CHAPTER 4

The Cost of Living

Part One: A Place to Live. When you are budgeting your money, the largest expense for almost everyone is their home. It doesn't matter if you are renting a home or buying a home, paying for a place to live will typically require at least a quarter of your income every month; perhaps as much as a third of your income. As a rule of thumb, most financial advisors will recommend that you spend about 30% of your gross income on housing. This means someone making $100,000 a year ($8,333 a month) should spend no more than $30,000 a year ($2,500 a month) on housing.

The 30% rule of thumb deals with gross income (the total before taxes). When you look at how much of your money can go to housing after we account for taxes, it become more evident that this is a substantial expense. In the example, we have someone making $100,000 a year. For Social Security and Medicare, this person will pay the payroll tax of 7.65% on their wages ($7,650 for the year). For federal income taxes, we will assume this person is married and there for they can take a standard deduction of $30,000 on their income taxes, leaving $70,000 in taxable income. The places them in the 12% tax bracket, so their federal income taxes would be ($7,923 for the year). The total federal tax burden in this case is $15,573 a year. If we also assume this person live in Pennsylvania and must also pay 3.07% of their income (or $3,070) in state income tax each year. Their net income for the year, after subtracting $18,643 in state and federal taxes, is down to $81,357. This is still a very good income, but when we consider the cost of housing after taxes, we find that spending $30,000 a year for housing consumes more almost 37% of their net (after tax) income.

In this book we will look at living expenses across your career by examining how much the average American of the same age is spending and budgeting the same amount for you. By doing this, the model presented in this book allows you to enjoy the same lifestyle as your non-military contemporaries. For example, at the age of 20, the average American male makes $42,380 a year ($812 a week) and spends an average of $17,121 on housing.[32] We see that our youngest Americans are spending an average of 40% of their gross income on housing. The methodology used in this book finds the percentage of income spent on the various categories and recommends that you spend the same amount. This methodology will be used for all expenses – except housing. One of the most valuable benefits of military compensation is the housing allowance. Throughout your military career, you (and your dependents) will be provided housing at no cost, or you will be provided a housing allowance –the Basic Allowance for Housing, or BAH– to cover the cost of your housing.

Because housing costs vary significantly between locations, your BAH will vary based on your location. For example, an 18-year-old service member with no dependents assigned to duty in San Francisco would receive a housing allowance of $3,447 each month, while the same person assigned duty at Fort Leonard Wood, Missouri would receive less than one-third of that amount ($1,119 a month) for housing. You likely also noticed that the housing allowance our 18-year-old service member is paid in San Francisco ($41,364 a year) is almost as much as the *total income* for the average 20-year-old American. BAH also increases as your paygrade increases. Using the examples above a married E-7 assigned to duty in San Francisco would receive a housing allowance of $5,353 each month, while the same person assigned duty at Fort Leonard Wood, Missouri would receive $1,647 a month to house his family.

The military reevaluates BAH rates every year based on local price data for median local rental housing costs and average utility costs (including electricity, heating fuel, water, & sewer). Collecting nationwide rental housing cost data for approximately 300 locations across the United States that typically house more than 100 BAH recipients to ensure allowances reflects local market condition changes. Rental costs are collected for different types of rental units (i.e., apartments, townhouses/duplexes, and single-family homes of varying bedroom sizes). Rental housing costs are based on the average housing choices for civilians with similar incomes. Because BAH is based on housing costs in the local area, we do not need to calculate how much you should be spending on housing throughout your career; we can simply offer the one simple recommendation for housing throughout your career –and this recommendation is the same for all "allowances" received– spend the allowance on the expense it is intended to pay for. It is possible that you could find housing for an amount below your housing allowance, allowing you to pocket the excess, but that is a personal decision, and one may not be acceptable for many people. It is also possible that you may want to live in a house that costs more than the housing allowance; that is also a personal choice, but one that does impose a cost on your financial health in both the short-term and the long-term. Does a single 19-year-old, need to live in a two-bedroom single family home? No. They may want to "live large," but a one-bedroom apartment is more than sufficient and spending more on housing to live a more lavish lifestyle when you are young will force you to live a more modest lifestyle in your later years. For your housing, you should accept the free housing offered by the government –if it is available– or use your housing allowance to pay for your housing.

Before we conclude this discussion of housing, a few points about government housing ("on post" or "on base" housing) and your housing allowance are worth noting. First, as mentioned previously, BAH rates are adjusted every year. They typically go up, but they can go down. Imagine that you move to a base and your BAH at the new location is

$2,000 a month, so you sign a lease to rent a townhouse for $1,800 a month (you remembered that your rent payment is not your only housing expense, so you allowed $300 of your BAH to pay for utilities). The next year the local housing market crashes and the BAH rate for your location drops to $1,750. How are you going to pay your housing bills (rent AND utilities)?! Fear not. The military understands that you likely signed a contractual obligation to pay some amount every month based on the BAH rates in effect when you arrived at a duty location; for this reason, your BAH will never be reduced while you remain at that location. However, if BAH rates are adjusted upwards, you will receive the increase. Again, unless you move to a new location, your BAH can go up, but it will never go down.

Related to the annual adjustment of BAH rates, is a second important consideration: the concept of "paying" for government housing. There are a number of different ways that the military provides housing for military members and their families. At the very start of your career (basic training), you will live in a barracks ("dormitory" in Air Force parlance) at least until you finish your training. At your first duty station, if you have no dependents, you will probably continue to live in a barracks/dormitory. From a financial standpoint, this is ideal. Your housing is free and you commute to work is probably measured in steps rather than miles. When you get married, you will no longer be allowed to live in the barracks, so you will need to seek other living quarters. You may choose to remain "on base" and relocate to family housing. This has many of the same benefits as living in the barracks: you don't have any housing bills to pay and your commute is still relatively short. There are two primary types of "on base" housing: government housing and privatized housing. If your duty location offers government housing, you will have no housing bills to pay; the government provides your family with a home (and all utilities except TV, telephone and internet) at no cost to you. Because you are being provided with a home, you will obviously not receive a housing allowance. If your duty location offers "privatized" housing, this simply means that the government has hired a contractor (a civilian company) to manage housing. The key differences will be that in privatized housing, you will receive a housing allowance from the government, but 100% of this money will need to be paid to the contractor (this can be done through payroll deduction, known as an "allotment"). You will also not have a water bill, electric bill, etc. in privatized housing, but you may find that the contractor offers some incentive to reduce energy use. This typically involves you receiving some refund of the BAH you paid to the contractor if your energy usage is lower than the average usage in your housing area. If you choose not to live in government housing (or if government housing is not available), you will be paid BAH. BAH is comprehensive (covering rent *and* utilities), although it does not cover not-housing expenses such as telephone, television, or internet service, but it is intended to cover only 95% of your total housing expenses. The implications of this will be discussed later.

Again, throughout your military career, you will enjoy housing at no cost, or you will be provided a housing allowance to pay for your housing. This is an amazing financial advantage of military service. Enjoy it!

Part Two: Something to Eat. Everyone has to eat! Fortunately for you, the military provides you with all of your meals, or an allowance to feed yourself. In 2025, that allowance is $465.77 a month. If we compare that to the average American, we find the average 20-year-old American male (again, having an average income of $42,380 a year) spends $4,787 a year (or $398.92 a month) on food.[33]

Your Basic Allowance for Subsistence (BAS), like BAH is an "allowance." This means it is money provided to you for a specific purpose; in this case: food. It also means this money is not subject to being taxed. As with all allowances, you should spend all of this money for its intended purpose. If you find that you –like the average American 20-year-old– don't need to spend all of this money on food, you should invest any excess into your retirement savings.

Your BAS is for *you*. Although your housing allowance changes when you get married (or otherwise acquire dependents), your BAS will not change. The reasoning here is quite simple. The military is committing to providing food and shelter to all service members. If they aren't providing you with meals and housing (known as "in kind"), they will provide you with tax-free money to acquire your own meals and your own housing. The military has no obligation to provide meals and lodging to your family. The military chose to have a relationship with you. You chose to have a relationship with your family (the military didn't "get a vote"). However, the military understands that in providing you with a place to live, you likely want to live with your spouse, etc. As a result, the do provide an allowance that provides housing for you with the understanding that your family will need to live there as well.

Related to the idea of the military providing food for the service member, but not their families, is the idea of military members participating in the government's Supplemental Nutrition Assistance Program ("Food Stamps"). The bottom line is this: it is only in extremely rare circumstances that a member of the military would qualify for food stamps. In 2025, a single person cannot make more than $1,632 a month to be eligible for food stamps. The lowest paid person in the military (an E-1, with less than four months of service makes more than this in basic pay. . . and they have their meals and housing provided at no cost! No single person in the military can ever qualify for food stamps, so let's look at families.

A family of two cannot make more than $2,215 a month to be eligible for food stamps. The lowest paid E-2 (someone with six months in the military) still makes more than this in basic pay and, again, they have their meals and housing provided at no cost. Consider a married E-1 (the lowest pay grade), assigned to duty at Fort Leonard Wood, Missouri (we use this location because it has some of the lowest BAH rates in the country). This Soldier would receive basic pay of $2,108.10, BAH of $1,224 and BAS of $465.77 every month. That's a total of $3,797.87 every month (and a lot of it tax-free!). Although this is about the lowest compensation a married service member can earn, they are still making 166% of the maximum that a two-person household can earn and still be eligible for food stamps. What if they have a child? The $3,797.87 a month that our lowest paid married Soldier is making is still more than the qualifying threshold for food stamps (even if they have two kids). What if they have a lot of kids? Let us assume that our Fort Leonard Wood service member is promoted to E-3 on schedule (at one year of service) and has somehow managed to have three children in that same one-year span, we find his income is now $4,174 a month ($2,484.60 in basic pay, $1,224 in BAH and $465.77 in BAS). A married service member with three kids (a family of five) can make no more than $3,963 to qualify for food stamps; our Soldier with just one year of service still makes too much money even with a family of five. Let's say they have another baby. When this baby is born, our Soldier now has two years in the military (impressive that he has had four children in two years!) and is now an E-4 making $4,583 a month ($2,892.90 in basic pay, $1,224 in BAH and $465.77 in BAS). A married service member with four kids (a family of six) can make no more than $4,546 to qualify for food stamps. Our service member (and their spouse) have done incredible work to build their family so quickly, but they still make too much money to qualify for food stamps. Now consider the fact that the median income for high school graduates in the U.S. is only $41,420 a year ($3,452 a month), the average American household with three kids and only one (high-school-graduate-level) income likely qualifies for food stamps, but our service member does not.[34]

The reality is that it is in very rare circumstances that service members will be eligible for food stamps if they receive BAH and BAS (e.g., *very* large families at very low rank). News reports of service members on food stamps tug at the heartstrings, so you hear about them, but they are aberrations, typically the result of the fact that the government does not count the value of living in government housing for free in their calculations for food stamps. Free housing has value –and the military can easily put a dollar value on that benefit– but is not included in food stamp eligibility calculations.

Part Three: Transportation. Everyone needs a place to shelter from the weather, and Americans spend an average of 25% of their income on housing. Everyone needs to eat, and Americans spend an average of 10% of their income on food. It would be reasonable to conclude that Food and Shelter are the two biggest expenses for the average American; but that conclusion would be incorrect. After housing, the average American spends the most money on transportation, about 17% of their total expenditures.[35]

For most Americans a car is not a luxury, it is a necessity. Our society has developed around the idea of people living outside of urban centers (in the suburbs), and using cars to move between their home, their job, and the services they need in the community. In the very early days of your career (in basic training and then living in the barracks) you probably won't need a car. You will *want* one, but you probably won't *need* one. Nonetheless, before too long you will indeed need a car, and you should buy one!

Buying (or *not* buying) a car becomes more challenging because they can serve multiple purposes. A car can be used to take you across distances that you cannot easily cover on foot. A car can be used to move heavy loads (like groceries) over long distances. A car can be used to demonstrate your financial success or otherwise impress people. Some of these, but not all, are valid reasons to buy a car. If your house is more than a few miles away from your place of employment, you probably need a car. If you cannot reasonably carry a week's worth of groceries from the store to your house, you might need a car. If you want a car to impress other people, you probably don't need a car.

You have almost certainly been told that it is never financial prudent to buy a new car; this is absolutely true. A new car loses up to 30% of its value in the first year, and as much as 60% after five years.[36] You also know that financing a car is expensive. If you do need a car, the most financially responsible course of action is to but a good, reliable used car. If you buy a three-year-old car, rather than a new one, you are getting reliable transportation and allowing someone else to pay for the depreciation. You can look around and guess that everyone except you is driving a new car. That is not the case. You tend to focus on the flashy new car one friend bought because it is eye-catching. The reality is that the average vehicle on the road in the United States is almost 13 years old.[37] If you buy a car that is five years-old (letting someone else pay the 60% depreciation cost), then drive it for five years before selling it, you are still driving a car that is younger than the average car on the road. You can be financially smart and still live a better life than the average American!

Part Four: Staying Healthy (Medical and Dental Insurance). You need medical and dental coverage, everyone does. You will receive comprehensive medical and dental treatment at absolutely **no cost**! No matter what happens to you while you are in uniform, you will be treated. All your treatments, surgeries, prescriptions, etc. are provided. Your dental care is entirely free too.

When you do start a family, they will also benefit from the military healthcare system. At most military bases, your family members can be seen at the Military Treatment Facility (MTF) at no cost. Dental insurance is also offered for military family members; for a spouse, this will cost you $12.10; if you have a larger family, your cost will be $31.46 a month.

If your family members need to be seen at a civilian medical facility, they will be covered by Tricare, the military's healthcare insurance program. You will have the option to enroll your family in "Tricare Prime" or Tricare Select" (all service members are automatically enrolled in Tricare Prime). Service members enrolled in Tricare Prime will never have to pay any bills and their family members enrolled in Prime will only have small co-payments; this is an incredibly affordable healthcare insurance program. Tricare Select does have an annual deductible and a 20% cost share for outpatient care, but it has a Maximum Out Of Pocket (MOOP) cost of $1,000; this means a family enrolled in Tricare select will never pay more than $1,000 for medical care in any given year.

The big question is, how do you know how much Tricare is worth to you? One way to measure this is to see how much it would cost you to buy Tricare Select coverage without the military paying for any of it. This option exists as the Continued Health Care Benefit Program (CHCBP), which is essentially the civilian version of Tricare Select; like Tricare, it is managed by Humana. In 2016, CHCBP premiums were $1,372 per quarter for individual coverage and $3,087 per quarter for family coverage. In addition to these premiums, there will be yearly deductibles and cost-shares similar to Tricare Select. That comes out to **a minimum of $5,488 (individual) or $12,348 (family) respectively a year**. Plus, consider that is also a tax-free benefit so it's worth even more than just an equivalent cash payout.[38]

CHAPTER 5

The Military Millionaire Model

Life is the result of the choices you make. The model presented here assumes you live a life that parallels the average American (same level of spending, same age at marriage, same number of children, *et cetera*). You could life a different life. You could life a more spartan life than your peers. You could get married later in life. You could focus on your career and get promoted earlier than your peers. All these choices would result in you having more wealth that the example presented in this book. Conversely, you could choose to spend more than other Americans of your age, and/or get married earlier than most Americans, *et cetera*. These choices would likely result in you having less wealth than the example shown in this book. Again, **the model presented here does not require you to have a lower quality of life than your peers**.

The Basics of Investing

Risk and Reward. Think of investing this way: If you take $10 and bury it in your backyard, what are the odds that you will find only $5 when you dig it up a year later? Zero. Your money is absolutely safe, it will still be exactly $10 a year later. You have taken no risk and therefore you have not lost anything. But you have also not gained anything (no reward). Now, take that same $10 and loan $2 each to five of your friends. They each agree to pay you $3 nest year. So, you loan out your $10 to five friends and sit back for a year just waiting to collect you $15. Unfortunately, you did accept some risk; although your friends are all good people and fully intend to pay you back at the end of that year, one of them is lost in the ice while climbing Mount Everest. At the end of the year, only four of your friends are able to repay the loan, so you finish with $12. You took some risk, and as a result, you have $2 more than if you had buried your money in the back yard. The bottom line: more risk provides greater return. If you bought stock in Apple when it was new, you would be taking a lot of risk by investing in an unknown and unproven company. I'm sure you're aware that risk has paid off; $1.00 worth of Apple stock in 1985 is worth more than $2,000 today. Great risk produced great reward. If you invested in Apple in 2025 – when the company is well known and there is little risk it will go bankrupt or that it's products won't be wanted – a year later, your shares will probably be worth about what you paid for them. Little risk, little reward.

Risk is tied to reward, but risk also equals risk. Taking a risk (like investing in a new company) can produce great rewards. But you must always remember that taking a risk is, of course, risky. If – instead of Apple – you had chosen to invest your money in Blockbuster, your money would all have vanished. But you can manage your *risk exposure* by not investing in Blockbuster, or even Apple. . . exclusively. If we return to the example of loaning $10 to your friends, if you gave all $10 of your money to one friend, with the agreement that they pay you $15 at the end of the year, you might have done alright. . . unless the one friend you chose to invest in was the Mount Everest explorer who never returned to repay you (the "Blockbuster Video" of your investment portfolio). The key to success is to avoid giving all of your money to one friend. You need to give your money to a diverse group of friends. This is "**diversification**." If one of your friends falls off the earth, you still have other friends you can count on. If you invested in Blockbuster *and* Apple, you would be a wealthy person, and you would have reduced your risk by diversifying your investments rather than betting all your money on one horse. We'll touch on diversification again in a moment.

Where should I invest my money? TSP. That's it. A one-word answer (actually, a three-word answer). The TSP ("Thrift Savings Plan") is the cornerstone of the wealth creation plan laid out in this book. The TSP is the government equivalent of a civilian 401(k) retirement plan. The term "401(k)" might seems intimidating; it shouldn't be. This is simply where you can find the law that allows you to save part of your income for retirement and receive special tax treatment for that money; think of it as nothing more than a paragraph number in the U.S. tax code (specifically, subsection (k) of section 401 of Title 26 of the United States Code). The terms TSP and 401(k) are essentially interchangeable with the sole caveat that only government employees (e.g., the military) can participate in the TSP.

One great benefit of the TSP is the government "matching funds." If you contribute 5% of your pay to your TSP account, the government will also contribute 5%. This means if you are contributing 5% of your base pay, the government will contribute the same amount to your TSP account. This is, in essence a free pay raise from the government, just for taking advantage of the TSP program! Right from the start of your career, you can give yourself a pay raise of more than $1,000 a year just by putting that amount into your TSP. If you follow the plan laid out in the following chapters, your contributions and the government matching funds mean you will have a more than $10,000 in your TSP in the first year. Get the free pay raise the government is offering you!

Investing in the TSP also has tax advantages. If you invest in a "Roth" TSP account, you pay tax on your income now, but when you take those dollars out of the TSP in retirement, you will owe no taxes. Some people may be tempted to but their money into a "traditional" (non-Roth) TSP plan. The advantage of doing this is that your contributions to a "traditional" retirement plan are made with "pre-tax" dollars, which reduces the income taxes you owe for the year you make the contribution. To illustrate how this works, consider the $9,898 that this book will recommend you contribute to the TSP during your first year in the military. Soldier Smarte puts her $9,898 into a "Roth" TSP; Airman Thicke puts his $9,898 into a "traditional" TSP. At the end of the year they each file their income taxes. You might assume –because they both have exactly the same income– that they both owe the same amount of income tax; this is not the case. Because Airman Thicke contributed to a "traditional" TSP, his contributions are "pre-tax" (this money goes into the TSP before it can be counted in your income for the year). This means that when he files his taxes, he has $9,898 less taxable income than Soldier Smarte. Because both Soldier Smarte and Airman Thicke are in the 10% tax bracket, Airman Thicke's income tax bill will be $990 less that Soldier Smarte's income tax bill. You can imagine that Airman Thicke feels pretty proud of himself when he tells everyone that he is getting a $990 income tax refund – especially when he learns that Soldier Smarte is getting no refund at all. Every year for the next 30 years, Airman Thicke puts the same amount ($9,898) in a traditional TSP, and gets a $990 tax refund. Every year for the next 30 years, Soldier Smarte puts the same amount in a Roth TSP, and gets a $0 tax refund. Over this 30-year period, Airman Thicke has gotten an extra $29,700 in tax refunds ($990 x 30 years) that Soldier Smarte didn't get. Should we be like Airman Thicke and contribute to a traditional TSP plan? No! Because we will retire at some point and want to take the money out of our TSP, we need to consider how that works out for Airman Thicke and Soldier Smarte. After 30 years, they both have the same amount in their TSP ($1.9 million, assuming their TSP investments grew by 8.35% every year).

Both Thicke and Smarte are retired and receiving a military pension (putting them in the 12% tax bracket). When Airman Thicke withdraws $25,000 from his TSP, he learns he will only be getting $22,000 because the other $3,000 is being sent to the Internal Revenue Service to cover the taxes on the $25,000 in income his TSP withdrawal represents. When Soldier Smarte withdraws the same $25,000, she gets the entire $25,000 because she paid the tax on their TSP over the last 30 years. Airman Thicke *thought* he was the intelligent one because he saved $990 a year in taxes over his 30-year career; totaling $29,700 that Soldier Smarte didn't get. But Soldier Smarte gets to keep all $25,000 a year that she withdrawals from her Roth TSP, but Thicke only gets to keep $22,000 of the $25,000 he withdrawals from his traditional TSP. As Soldier Smarte goes through her 30-year retirement, she *knows* she was the smart one because the money Airman Thicke saved in taxes will be a lot less than the $90,000 she will save in taxes on her $25,000 withdrawals each year for the next 30 years.

In retirement, Airman Thicke now has to pay taxes on the contributions that weren't taxed during his career (because "traditional" retirement plans aren't taxed until the retiree takes the money out), but he also has to pay tax on any money that he has earned on his investments. Conversely, Soldier Smarte paid taxes on her contributions during his career, but she can now make withdrawals without having to pay any tax. She paid taxes on her contributions when she made the deposits, but the money she has earned on her investments is never taxed (because "Roth" retirement plans both contributions and earnings are tax-free when the retiree takes the money out (after the age of 59½). Additionally, it is very likely that your income will be higher in retirement than it is early in your career; this means you will be in a higher tax bracket when you take withdrawals from your TSP than you were in when you made the contributions. When you retire as a millionaire, your taxes will almost certainly be much higher than they are now.

Where, in the TSP, should I invest my money? Okay, so you're committed to investing in the TSP, but which fund *within the TSP* should get your money? This is probably the most intimidating part of this entire plan, but there is no need to be scared. This really is very easy to understand. The TSP has 16 different funds that you can choose to invest in. If you don't make a choice, the plan will put your money in the "G Fund." The "G" is short for government, you are essentially investing in the U.S. government. This is a very safe investment; it is very unlikely that you will ever lose money by investing in the G Fund. However, the money that you do make isn't going to be great. Because there is very little risk, there is very little return. Before you decide which fund is right for you, you need to consider risk and what your personal tolerance for risk. You also need to remember how diversification can mitigate risk. Fortunately, the TSP makes diversification easy. Let's look at each of the TSP funds and what you are buying when you invest in them.

Understanding the TSP Funds. Five of the TSP funds invest in stocks and bonds. By buying stocks (partial ownership of a company – like Apple) and bonds (a loan to a company or government – like your loan to your friends), these funds gain value when the companies they have invested in grow in value and when the loans they make to companies and governments through bonds are repaid with interest. Again, there is risk here because some of the companies that the funds purchases shares of may lose value. Similarly, some bond issuers may default (not pay) the payments due on the bonds; however, the funds are all diversified by investing in a large number of different stocks and bonds.

- <u>G Fund</u>. The default investment in the TSP is the G Fund. This fund is guaranteed by the U.S. government and pay interest that is based on the interest that the U.S. Treasury is paying to people who loan money to the U.S. government. Over the last thirty years, the return on the G Fund has been about 4 percent per year; that is, $100 put into the G Fund would be worth about $104 a year later. Very safe, but relatively low return.

- C Fund. The C Fund ("C" for "Common Stock") invests in large medium-sized American businesses. These are the companies that everyone is relatively familiar with, like Tesla and Apple (two of the top 10 holding in the C Fund in March of 2021). Over the last thirty years, the return on the C Fund has been about 11 percent per year; that is, $100 put into the G Fund would be worth about $111 a year later. Good return (almost three times as much as the G Fund), but more risk (in 2018 the C Fund ***lost*** almost 7% of its value; that same year the G Fund still gained about 3%).
- S Fund. The S Fund ("S" for "Small") invests in small to medium-sized American businesses. In this case "small" does not mean a lemonade stand or your friend who makes screen-printed T-shirts in his basement. It also does not mean Microsoft or Ford. Think more like Uber and Lululemon (two of the top 10 holding in the S Fund in March of 2021). These investments bring more risk than the C Fund, but the potential for greater returns. In the year ending March of 2021, the S fund returned 60% ($100 invested in 2020 would be worth $160 in 2021); almost twice the 34% gain in the C Fund during the same time. Conversely during the 2018 fall that dropped the C Fund by 7%, the S Fund lost almost twice as much value (11%).
- I Fund. The I Fund ("I" for "International") is much like the C Fund, except it invests in international businesses (like Toyota). Over the last thirty years, the return on the I Fund has been about 6 percent per year; that is, $100 put into the G Fund would be worth about $106 a year later. A fair return for a fair level of risk.
- F Fund. Unlike the C, S and I Funds, the F Fund ("F" for "Fixed Income") does not invest in stocks. This fund is more like the G Fund, seeking to profit from fixed income investments (like the loans to your friends – you loan them money and they agree to pay you back at a specified interest rate). Over the last thirty years,

> the return on the F Fund has been about 6 percent per year; that is, $100 put into the G Fund would be worth about $106 a year later. A fair return with limited risk.

Obviously, we all want to have all of our money invested in the S Fund during the years when it is returning 60%, but none during the years when it is losing money. Similarly, we want to have all of our money in the G Fund when every other fund is losing money, but may regret having any money in the G Fund when every other fund is making twice as much money. This, quite simply, can't be done. No one can "time the market." Don't try, you will lose. But never fear, we can use time to help us continue to grow our wealth despite the ups and downs in the stock markets.

The first thing working in our favor is the benefit of time. If you have $1000 invested in a fund that loses 10% for the year, you finish the year with $900. It hurts, but if you never add another penny to that fund, and it grows 10% the next year, you will finish year two with $990. After two years, you're still not back where you started, but if we average 10% gains for the rest of a twenty-year career, the initial $1000 will be worth over $5500, despite losing 10% early on. Time has value (more on this later).

The second thing that you can take advantage of are the other TSP funds, called "Lifecycle" funds or "L Funds." These funds invest your money in a mix of all five of the funds mentioned above. Early on, they will have a lot of money in the funds with more risk (and, importantly, more return). As time goes by and you get closer to retirement, the funds will gradually (automatically every quarter) shift more of your money into the lower risk investments to protect the gains you made by accept more risk when you were younger. The funds each have a number after them indicating the year that the fund expects participants to stop adding money and start withdrawing money. For example, the L2065 Fund is designed for the person who expects to begin withdrawing funds in 2063 or later; because this is 40 years in the future, the fund has most of its money (49%, as of January 2021) in the C Fund, and less than 1% in the G Fund. Conversely, people who have had their money in the L2025 Fund, have experienced their years of growth and are now probably more concerned with protecting the wealth they have grown. Hence, the L2025 Fund has 46% of its money in the safe G Fund, but only 6% in the S Fund. You can use the "L" funds to manage your mix of investments for you!

Your "risk tolerance" is going to determine the right fund for you. If you are comfortable with the possibility of losing money (perhaps a lot of money) some years, you may be more interested in the C, S and/or I Funds. If you couldn't bear the thought of finishing a year with less money that you had at the start of the year, you probably want to stick with the G Fund or the F Fund. If you want to have someone else decide what the right mix of investments is, you may want an L Fund. Again, your risk tolerance is personal to you. Only you know the right investment for you. For simplicity, the examples presented in this book will assume the service member in vested in a Lifecycle "L" Fund with a target date 45 years in the future (when they would approach retirement age).

Where Do I Get the Money to Invest? "I don't make enough to invest!" Most new service members, like most Americans, will say: "I don't make enough to save for retirement" or "I need to feed my family today; I can't worry about thirty years from now!" This is perhaps the fundamental barrier that prevents most Americans from achieving financial independence. Obviously, if you spend all your money as you earn it, you'll have a better lifestyle today than someone who saves some of their money. But when your salary stops (and it always does), you will need to start living off what you've saved over your career. Once you retire, the tables will turn. The person who saved a little each month will have a much nicer lifestyle than the person who spent everything they made throughout their career.

Even worse, you could spend all your money, and use credit cards to spend even more money than you make. Yes, you could have a very nice life indeed. . . until you don't. Remember the example of the former professional athlete at the soup kitchen? Credit cards are the middle-class equivalent of that tale. As noted previously, there are two kinds of people: 1) those that spend money, and 2) those that have money. The person who spends every cent they make during their working life, will have to work until they die. The person who saves and invests smartly, will retire early and truly enjoy life.

"I'm an E-1. I don't make enough to invest!"

Years ago, when the government used conscription (a "draft") to fill the ranks of the military, there was little need to offer high pay to people serving in uniform because the government could compel as many people as needed to fill the ranks. If we look at the "starting salary" of a service member in 1965, we find they made $93.90 each month (or $1,127 a year). The average non-military wage earner in 1965 made $4,915 – more than four time as much.[39] It would be hard to argue that the military were "well paid" in 1965. However, what was true in 1965 is not true today. The reality is that since the United States abandoned military conscription ("the draft"), the military has needed to pay a market wage to attract and retain the talent it needs. As you will see laid out through each step that follows in this book, today's military not only pays as well as the "civilian world," *it pays more*. That "more" that the military pays service members is the key to living the same lifestyle as the average American while building a million-dollar fortune (or more). Using data from various sources, this book will make it clear that military compensation is superior to the compensation paid to most Americans outside the military.

The "right" or "wrong" of that circumstance is outside the scope of this book. This book is about finance. Numbers. Facts. This book is not arguing that the level of military compensation is either appropriate or inappropriate. It is what it is, and it is good. It is true, however, that although some of the hardships linked to military service are shared by some outside the military, the women and men who serve in the military endure hardships that most Americans do not. Some business professionals are required to spend a lot of time away from the family and friends. Similarly, the mortal danger than can accompany military service also exists in the professional lives of policemen, firefighters and others. It is unlikely, however, that any occupation outside of the military entails all of the hardships involved in military service. It is also true that the military only accepts the very best. The Department of Defense's "Qualified Military Availability" study from 2020 estimates that only about 23% of Americans aged 17 to 24-years meet the criteria to serve in the military.

"Live within your Means"

You do not need to "scrimp and save" to become wealthy in the military. This book will show you how you can live the 'average' American lifestyle and just invest the extra pay –above what the average American earns–that the military provides. Serving a career in the military can allow you to have the same standard of living as other Americans *and* get wealthy. While serving in the military, you could also choose to have a higher standard of living than the average American and *not* become wealthy. The key to building wealth is to "live within your means." Don't spend everything you earn, and absolutely do not spend *more* than you earn!

How could I possibly spend more than I earn? Most of you probably know the answer to that question (credit cards and other uses of credit such as loans). Credit cards and loans are not "bad," but that can cause serious problems if you misuse them. If you have a credit card with no annual fee (and you should), and you pay of the entire balance every month (and you should), credit cards can offer many benefits at no cost. Credit cards allow you the freedom to go about your day-to-day life without worrying about keeping enough cash in your wallet. Credit cards can also earn you "free" money. If you have a card that offers you "cash back" and you spend $100 on groceries and $50 on gas every month, your credit card you earn you $1.50 every month (assuming a 1% cash back rate). Now $1.50 isn't a lot of money, but over the course of a year that amounts to almost $20 in "free money." I'll admit that even $20 isn't a life-changing amount of money, but I would still cross the street to pick up a $20 bill and using a cash back credit card requires even less effort to get the money.

The two keys to using a credit card "safely" are to: 1) ***always pay it off every month***, and 2) ***don't pay an annual fee***. If you don't pay off you balance in full every month, you can start to make the credit card company very rich and your family very poor. Let's go back to the example of charging $100 for groceries and $50 for gas in a month. If you only pay the minimum payment (let's say $25), the unpaid balance begins to charge interest. Your $150 in credit used, minus the $25 you paid, leaves a $125 balance owed to the credit card company. If we assume your credit card is like most, it will probably charge about 18% interest on the unpaid balance. So next month, you find that you now owe the credit card company about $127. If you only make the minimum payment ($25) again you continue to accrue more interest charges and it will take you six months to pay off the credit card and cost you almost $6 in interest. Now, $6.00 isn't a staggering amount of money, but in this example we only charged $150 in goods one month, and never used the card again. If we assume you have a $5,000 credit limit on your card and you continue to spend $150 a month and only make the minimum payments, you would reach your credit limit in less than three years (31 months); now you can no longer use the card. In those 31 months, you would have charged $4,650 in gas and groceries. For that you have made payment of $750 ($25/month x 30 months). You charged $4,650 and paid $750; Your charges, minus your payments equals $3,900, but you don't owe the credit card company $3,900, you owe them $4,975! You've already paid the credit card company $750 and you still owe them more than the cost of everything you every bought. That's bad. . . and it gets worse. . . .

If you continue to pay the minimum payment, you will *NEVER* pay off your debt. The balance you owe is now costing you almost $75 every month just in interest charges. If you now triple your payment and start paying the credit card company $75 every month, it will only take you another *thirty years* to pay off your credit card. When you do finally pay off your credit card (long after you have retired from the military, and thirty years after you last used it), the $4,650 in gas and groceries you charged decades ago will have cost you more than $27,000!!! Yes, you paid almost $30,000 for less than $5,000 in gas and groceries.

Think of it this way: you started using the card when you were 18 years old; you hit your credit limit before your turned 21. We assume you never charged anything ever again and you still had to pay a credit card bill after you turned 50 years old. That is a life-long burden that came from not paying for you gas and groceries when you were a teenager.

Not only has your "bad" use of credit cost you more than $20,000 in interest fees and a lifetime of stress, it has also impacted your credit score. Because you used all of the credit available to you, your credit score will be very low. Who cares? You do! The lower your credit score, the more you pay to borrow money. If you tried to get a second credit card, it wouldn't charge the same 18% interest as the first card; it is more likely to charge 20% interest (or more) and will probably have an annual fee as well. If you try to get a loan to buy a car, you will also pay more here too. You won't get the "0% financing" available to "qualified customers." You may find yourself paying 10% interest (or more) for your car loan. So the car you bought for $40,000 will actually cost you more than $51,000. That is, in essence another $11,000 that you have to pay because you didn't pay off your credit card in full every month.

The depressing examples may have you thinking "Well, I just wouldn't pay the credit card company. I'll keep the $20,000 in interest payments for myself and let them cancel the credit card." If you thought carrying a balance on your credit card did bad things to your credit rating, hold on, this is going to get rough!

Carrying a high balance on your credit card(s) hurts your credit rating; failing to pay your bills *kills* your credit rating. If you default on paying a debt (like your credit card) your credit rating will plummet. In this case, when you want a loan to buy a car, you won't get it. No loan. . . no car. Paying $51,000 for a $40,000 car because you have low credit sucks, but having to drive a $300 car –that breaks down every week– because you have *no credit* is worse. If you do find someone who is willing to give you a car loan, don't be surprised if the interest rate is more than 20%. That means you are now going to pay more than $60,000 for a $40,000 car (perhaps you should have just given that extra $20,000 to the credit card company).

If you aren't prudent in your use of credit, you can do a lot of damage. The previous examples should convince you that you don't want to misuse your credit. Again, ***always pay off your credit card every month***, and ***never use a card that charges an annual fee***.

Good use of credit. Now that we have seen the devastation credit cards can cause, let's look at the good they can do for you. As mentioned earlier, credit cards can just make your day-to-day life simpler; they can also make you a little bit richer. Returning to our same credit use scenario of $100 for groceries and $50 for gas every month, using a card that pays 1% cash back would "earn" you $18 every year. In reality, you could earn much more. If you simply charge all of your groceries (and use the $386.50 the military pays you to buy food every month to pay for it) over a 24-year military career that's more than $1000 in "free" money just for using a cash-back credit card to buy all of your groceries. Obviously if you charge even more, you get more rewards. You probably won't be able to pay your rent with a credit card without having to pay fees that would be more than any "cash back" you might get from your credit card, but you could charge other routine expenses (like your electric bill, for example) and earn even more. The key point in using a cash back credit card is to ensure you pay off the full balance every month. If you carry a balance, the interest that you will pay is almost certainly going to cost you more than any cash back you might get.

Another way that you can use a credit card for your benefit is building a positive credit history. You get a credit card with no annual fee and simply put it in a drawer and never use it. Just having a credit card will help build you credit history and improve your credit score, but remember, a missed payment will undone any positive effect that having the credit card may have had on your credit score. Similarly, if you carry a balance on the card from month to month, it will also have negative impact on your credit score.

Delayed Gratification

Closely linked to the idea of "living within your means" is the idea of "delayed gratification." Any plan that truly leads to wealth requires patience. People who can envision their future selves enjoying the benefits of the investments they make today are much more likely to succeed in the effort to become wealthy. This concept is called "delayed gratification."

Most Americans fall into one of two groups:
1) people who *spend* money people, or
2) who *have* money.

Let's consider two twin brothers in high school. Both have exactly the same resources (money, clothing, *et cetera*). Both brothers receive $100 for their birthday. One brother buys a new pair of shoes; the other brother buys nothing. When they go to school the next day, many of their classmates notice the one brother has new shoes and the other does not. They may be thinking the parents love the boy with new shoes more than his brother, or maybe he got a better job. In any case, most of the kids at school will think the boy with new shoes is better off than his brother who is wearing old shoes. The reality is, in fact, the opposite is true. Although the brother who bought the shoes has new shoes, his brother invested his $100 and is already richer than his brother because his $100 investment –even before any growth has occurred– is still worth $100, while his brother only has a pair of shoes that are worth less than $100 now that he has worn them.

Over time, that $100 that was invested will likely earn about the same return that the stock market has produced over the last 20 years. At the end of 20 years, the first brother has a very old (worthless) pair of shoes, but the investing brother has almost seven times as much money ($674) as he started with.[40] Even after we adjust for inflation, he still has almost five times as much money ($464) as he began with; his brother simply has a pair of worthless shoes.[41]The net worth of the first brother is $0. The net worth of the second brother is almost $500, in today's dollars. The brother who invested his money could now buy the same $100 shoes, and a second spare pair, and a pair for his brother, and still have almost twice the money he started with left over! The kids in school may have thought the brother with new shoes was the one to envy, but the truth is that the investing brother is the one who is building actual wealth. The first brother *spends* money; the second brother *has* money. Don't be fooled into thinking that you are "not doing as well as" your friends because they drive a newer car or have a bigger house. All you can tell from this kind of surface information is that they ***spend*** more money than you do. This doesn't mean they ***have*** more money than you do, in fact, ***they probably do not***.

The example of shoes may seem trivial, but the principle applies to every decision you make to spend or invest. Consider the same spending and investing twins buying cars. Both brothers have $50,000 to buy a car. The first brother spends $50,000 on a car. The second brother spends $15,000 on a good, reliable, three-year-old car. . . and invests the rest. The first brother has a nicer car but in 20 years when both brothers need to replace their cars, the first brother will have no money to buy another car. On the other hand, his investing brother will have almost a quarter million dollars ($337,000, or $232,000 adjusted for inflation) to buy a car. . . or maybe a house!

The brother who bought the new shoes and the nice new car enjoyed his money immediately. His brother who invested delayed gratification. He experienced less "joy" than his brother when they each first got the money, but in the long term, his investments offer him the opportunity to experience much more "joy" than his spending brother.

It would be nice to be in both groups (spend money *and* have money), but for the vast majority of Americans, that will never be the case. Don't fall into the trap of thinking that you aren't succeeding at life because you don't have the newest, nicest, most expensive anything. Unless you can look at someone else's bank account balances (actually, their investment portfolio), you don't know if they have any actual wealth. Indeed, a study by the Federal Reserve revealed that about 13 million American families have a *negative net worth* (the value of everything they have is less than what they owe to other people).[42] That is a lot of people who are good at spending but have not acquired *any* wealth.

One piece of wisdom that will help you achieve happiness as well as financial success: Comparison kills. People who spend their life looking at what other people have tend to be unhappy. Your neighbor with the nicer, newer car or a bigger house may create envy, but the reality is this probably means they have nothing saved. Like many Americans, they have a zero net worth. Enjoy what you have and know that you probably have a bigger pile of money that your neighbors who have chosen to be spenders rather than savers. Remember, people are typically not doing as well as it might seem; one in four American actually has a net worth of $0 or less![43]

You need to decide if you want to be a saver or a spender. The spender enjoys the thrill of a nice, new widget today, but never builds genuine wealth. The saver lives comfortably today – but not extravagantly– but grows genuine wealth. The saver will grow the wealth needed to allow them to enjoy financial independence later in life. . .

while their spending counterparts will need to work until they die (or have a much lower quality of life in retirement).

"See the big picture"

A dollar that you must give away is not real income. If Jim is paid $1,000 a month and Jane is paid $2,000 a month, who has more disposable income? If all other factors are equal, Jane clearly has more income. Unfortunately, this is typically as far as most people go in making these sorts of comparisons and they walk away thinking Jane has twice as much money as Jim. But we all know that "all other factors" are not always equal.

If we examine Jane and Jim in detail, we find that Jane must pay $400 in taxes, $500 in rent, $200 for food and $100 for health insurance. When these necessary expenses are accounted for, Jane has $800 left every month to spend as she chooses. We also learn that Jim must pay $150 in taxes (he's in a lower tax bracket than Jane because his taxable income is half that of Jane), his home is like Jane's, but provided by his employer at no cost to Jim. Similarly, Jim's meals and health insurance are also provided at no cost. At the end of each month, we see that Jim has $850 to spend as he chooses. Jim actually has more disposable income than Jane. The fool thinks that Jane's $2,000/month compensation is superior to Jim's compensation package, even though Jim's salary is only $1,000 a month. The wise person sees the bigger picture of compensation. If you can't see the big picture and understand the full value of your military compensation, the model shown in this book will not make sense to you.

CHAPTER 6

Assumptions

The model laid out in the previous chapter, and described in detail in subsequent chapters, involves a number of assumptions about you and the path your life will take. In every case, the assumptions are based on the "average" American. The model assumes your life will follow the course and timing of the majority of Americans. When necessary, the model also defaults to the assumption that is most *disadvantageous* to the military member in the model. For example, the model assumes that your spouse will only work until your first child is born. We know that the average American family of three (two parents and one child) has two breadwinners. Your spouse may or may not continue to earn an income after children come into the home; this book assumes they will not. Similarly, we assume that you will not be promoted faster than the average and that you will not be promoted to the highest ranks. Both of these are certainly possible –and both would certainly help you to build more wealth– but both are not going to be true for most people. The point here is that the model presented is not looking at your career and your financial life through rose colored glasses. The model assumes you are "average," no better; no worse.

Your Spouse (and their Income). Most of you will get married. In 2022, the average American man got married at the age of 30.[44] If you enlist in the military at the age of 18, you would be 12 years into your career when you get married. The examples in this book assume you are average, getting married at the age of 30. At this age you are 12 years into your military career and have been promoted to the pay grade of E-6.

Most of your spouses will work outside of the home. The examples presented in this book assume your spouse only earns an income during the first year of your marriage (until children enter the family). In practice, this means if you spouse is working outside the home, you can spend 100% of your spouse's disposable income on luxuries and still achieve the goal of becoming a millionaire using your military income only.

Not needing to rely on your spouse's income to have a comfortable lifestyle while still saving for a secure future may sound like a great thing; however, the financial benefits of having a second bread winner in the family are often not as great as you would imagine. Two key factors limit the financial benefits you might derive from being a two-income family: taxes and childcare expenses.

While not everyone may have children (and therefore childcare expenses), the requirement to pay tax on a spouse's income will apply to everyone. A very simple example will illustrate the income tax burden of a second income. As an E-6 your annual basic pay (the only part of your military compensation on which you must pay income tax) would be $58,306. After taking the standard deduction ($30,000 for married couples filing a joint return), your taxable income from serving in the military is $28,306. This would put you in the 10% tax bracket and your tax bill would be $2,831. So, you're paying $2,831 in federal income tax on a total basic pay of $58,306; you are only giving 4.85% percent of your taxable income to the government.

If your spouse takes job working for $15 an hour, their full-time wages for the year would add $31,200 to your family income. When we add this to your annual basic pay your combined income is now $89,506. After taking the standard deduction, your taxable income is $59,506 (The $28,306 that you are taxed on and the $31,200 your spouse added). This now puts you in the 12% tax bracket and your tax bill would be $7,141. Your tax bill has nearly tripled. You are paying another $4,310 on the $31,200 your spouse made (13.8%). You spouse has, after taxes, added $24,504 to the family budget ($31,200 minus $4,310 in federal income tax, $1934 in Social Security tax and $452 in Medicare tax).

No one is going to complain about having another $25,000 to play with. However, if (or when) you have children, the second factor that limits the financial value of a second income (childcare expenses) begins to show its ugly head. At your income level, you likely won't qualify for any government assistance; you and your spouse would pay an average of $16,000 a year for childcare.[45] When we take that $16,000 expense away from the $24,504 in additional disposable income, we find that your spouse is actually earning a net disposable income of $8,504 *a year*! That's equivalent to $4.09 an hour. There are few jobs that offer enough inherent joy that many people would do them if they realized they were getting less than $33 in spendable income for eight hours of work. In fact, if you consider the costs associated with working (clothes, gasoline for the commute, extra meals outside the home, *et cetera*), it is not unrealistic to think that your spouse may actually be *paying to have a job*. One large specialty coffee on the way to work, lunch at a restaurant near work and one gallon of gasoline for the daily commute day could wipe out all $32.70 of disposable income earned every day.

"Rate of Return." What do you get for investing your money? Every investment (TSP or otherwise) will have a variable rate of return, and this will change on an almost constant basis. We can, however, look at long-term averages to get a sense for the relative performance of different investment options. The TSP Fund (or Funds) you choose to invest in will depend or the level of risk you are willing to accept. In general, people are willing to accept more risk when they are younger, but want more security as they get older. This is the basic philosophy of the TSP Lifecycle Funds. For this reason, the examples in this book will assume you invested in a TSP "L" Fund. Over the 10 year period ending in 2021, the L2030 fund has returned an average of 8.35% per year; this same rate of return will be applied to your example investments as we go through your career in the following pages.

Promotion Timelines. For the example career timeline used in this book, a rough average across the services is used. We assume promotion will occur on the following timeline: E-2 after 6 months, E-3 at one year, E-4 at two years, E-5 at 5 years, E-6 at 9.5 years, E-7 at 15 years. The additional assumption if that you will not be promoted to the grade of E-8 (or E-9). Most service members who stay in the military will be promoted regularly. Almost every E-1 will become and E-2; almost every E-2 will become an E-3; almost every E-3 will become an E-4; most E-4s will be promoted to E-5; most E-5s will be promoted to E-6. Indeed, most E-6s will ultimately be promoted to E-7. Promotion to E-7 (Sergeant First Class, Chief Petty Officer, Gunnery Sergeant, or Master Sergeant in the Air Force and Space Force) is considered the hallmark of a fully successful career. Promotion beyond that point is, however, reserved for the most exceptional service members. **We assume you will *not* be promoted higher than E-7**.

Cost of Housing. Remember that your Basic Allowance for Housing is intended to accommodate the whole family, not just the service member. If you have a family, you will get a larger allowance to house your family. Additionally, the amount of BAH you are paid varies to account for the local housing market being more (or less) expensive than the national average. These two factors allow us to **use BAH to account for your housing costs** because this money covers your housing cost, regardless of the relative cost of your local housing market. Because BAH adjusts to compensate for different housing markets, when we consider housing costs throughout this book, we will use national averages.

BAH is intended to cover only 95% of your housing costs if you live off base. Because of this, we will need to account for the 5% differential between your housing costs and your housing allowance. The average

American currently pays $2,021 a month for housing.[46] Calculating 5% of the average housing cost ($2,021 x 5%), we get a figure of $106; this figure will be used in the model that follows to ensure you have enough money set aside to cover all of your housing costs. This figure represents the average, and your situation will almost always differ from the average to some degree. You can determine how much you should be adding to your housing funds every month by simply taking your BAH payment and dividing that number by 19. For example, a married Army Staff Sergeant (E-6) assigned to duty at Fort Leonard Wood would receive $1,542 in BAH every month. If we divide this number by 19, we get $81.16. This is the amount that our Fort Leonard Wood Soldier would need to add to their housing budget to fully cover their costs. As in our example, you may find that this $106, in addition to your BAH, is more than you need to fully cover your housing cost; you may find it is not enough. In either case, you should adjust your TSP contributions to match your personal situation.

A Growing Family. Family is one of the great joys in life; it is one of the very few things that can truly be priceless. Family is priceless, but it has a price. Yes, you might build a bigger pile of money if you never have a family, but you may not be as "rich" as the person who has a loving family but a more modest pile of money. The plan that is laid out in this book in based on the assumption that **you will want a family, and money will need to be allocated for that purpose**. Obviously, everyone's journey will be different, but we can make use of averages. The average woman in the United States gets married at 28.6 years of age; the average man gets married at the age of 30.5 years.[47] The example career that is laid out in this book assumes that you join the military at the age of 19, so the example has you getting married about nine and a half years later (at the age of 28.6). It is also assumed that children begin entering the picture one year later. This plan also assumes that the service member is the sole income earner in the family – **any income your spouse brings to the family can be spent on a more comfortable lifestyle!**

Home Ownership. Military service usually requires you to move every few years, and sometimes overseas. The model here assumes you will not become a homeowner.

Cost of Food. At the very start of your career, you will eat all your meals in a military dining facility ("mess hall"), so you obviously don't have to spend any money on food. Later in your career you may stop eating in the mess hall (receiving meals "in-kind"); when this change occurs, you will start receiving a Basic Allowance for Subsistence (BAS), known as "separate rations" because you are eating your rations separate from the others in your organization. This allowance covers the cost of food for the service member; however, once you get married, we need to supplement your BAS with money from base pay to cover food costs for the family. This will reduce the amount of money you can invest for retirement.

Annual Pay Increases and Allowances. Because annual pay increases are intended to offset inflation, you cannot expect to use any of this money for investing; you will need to spend your annual pay increases to afford the increasing costs of goods and services over time. Because this money is not reasonably available for investing, it will not be discussed as part of this plan. The same rule applies to all "allowances": Uniform Allowance, Cost of Living Allowance (COLA), Family Separation Allowance, Overseas Housing Allowance (OHA), Move-in Housing Allowance (MIHA), and dislocation allowance. "Allowances" are given to you to offset specific expenses that you incur. **You need to spend this money to maintain your lifestyle**.

Actual Dollar Amounts. Related to the discussion of annual pay increases is the dollar values used throughout this book. All dollar figures used in the examples use the 2025 military pay chart. As you reach the higher ranks, the cumulative effect of several annual pay increases will likely make the amount you are actually paid higher than the numbers presented here (perhaps substantially higher). The actual numbers are less important than the principle of this book: "live the 'average' American lifestyle and invest the extra pay the military provides." To find how much that average American is earning, you can check the Bureau of Labor Statistics (BLS) data on median income about every five years. The BLS can also provide you with the information about how much the average American is spending in various categories (for example, housing, food, healthcare).

CHAPTER 7

Putting the Plan into Action: E-1

This is the most important chapter of the book, and the most important piece of this chapter is this: Start Investing NOW! The dollars that you invest now (today!) are worth so much more than the dollars that follow. There are two reasons for this. First, the money you invest today will literally be worth more. If you invest $100 today, it will be worth more than $1,800 in 30 years (This assumes your investment earns the same return as the Standard & Poor's 500 Index (S&P 500). Since expanding to 500 stocks in 1957 through the end of 2021, the S&P500 has produced an average annualized return of 10.15%). Conversely, 30 years from now, $100 will be worth exactly $100. The second reason that your earliest investments are the most valuable is because your early investment help to cause subsequent investments. The hardest part of building wealth is simply starting. Once you begin investing, you are taking the key steps to making investing a habit. Once investing becomes a habit, you will truly be on your way to financial independence.

As an E-1

Your starting point: $ 0 in your TSP investments
$ 0 in your Emergency Fund

Your actions:

Contribute 37% of your Basic Pay to the TSP

Your ending point: $4,957 in your TSP investments
$ 150 in your Emergency Fund

The previous chapters have helped you to decide where (within the Thrift Savings Plan) you should invest. Now you need to determine "how much" you should invest. As of 2025, the Internal Revenue Service allows Americans to deposit as much as $23,500 into their 401K each year (the TSP is a 401K plan). The IRS increases these contribution limits periodically to keep up with inflation. It is probably unrealistic to expect an E-1 to contribute this much to their retirement because, in 2025, they will only earn $28,810 in base pay during their first year in the military.

As a new member of the military, you cannot reasonably contribute the maximum to your retirement accounts, so what can you (or what should you) contribute? The premise of this book is that you, the service member, can live on the same income as their non-military counterparts are making while investing the money that you earn that is in excess to what your civilian peers are earning.

In 2024, the average American between the ages of 20 and 24 earned $784 per week, before taxes.[49] So your peers are earning a gross income of $3,397 a month, or $40,764 a year. Given that a new E-1 in the military is only receiving $28,810 in basic pay during their first year in service, how can they possibly contribute anything to retirement? On the surface, it appears that you, the new E-1, are making $12,000 a year *less than your civilian counterparts*. Fortunately, you have this book and you learned in the early chapters that this superficial comparison is terribly misleading.

As an E-1, your after-tax "base pay" is almost all *disposable income* (i.e., money "in the bank"). In 2025, base pay for an E-1 with fewer than four months of military service is $2,144 per month, after we deduct federal taxes ($89 for income taxes, $133 for Social Security, $31 for Medicare) and $1 for the Armed Forces Retirement Home (a mandatory deduction for all enlisted service members) this drops to $1,890. Although not required, it is prudent for any service member to take advantage of the Servicemembers Group Life Insurance (SGLI), purchasing $500,000 of life insurance will only cost you $30 per month. After deducting the SGLI premium, you are left with $1,860 in disposable income every month.

To put this in perspective, the average American between the ages of 20 and 24 gross income of $3,397 a month. To determine their "disposable income" (money that spend as they choose) in a way that is comparable to military compensation, we must take into account their costs for housing, food and healthcare (all of which are provided at no cost to service members). But first we need to subtract the taxes they owe on their income. Note that because all of their income is taxable, your civilian peers will pay significantly more in taxes every month than those in the military. Federal income taxes on an income of $3,397 a month equal $258; Social Security taxes will be $211 a month and Medicare will cost them $49 a month. After deducting federal taxes, their disposable income drops to $2,879 a month.

You cannot live without food and shelter. In the military, your housing is provided at no cost. For your peers outside the military, the average single-person in their 20's spends 40 percent of their gross income ($1,359) on housing.[50] After we deduct the cost of housing from the median income of the average young American, we find that your civilian peers are left with $1,520 per month.

When must now consider the cost of food. As a military member, your meals are provided at no cost to you. If you find yourself in a situation where the military cannot provide your meals "in kind," they will provide you with a subsistence allowance to cover that cost. Your civilian counterparts are spending 11.2 percent of their income on food every month; this works out to $378 being spent to feed themselves every month. This comparison reveals that the $465.77 in BAS that you receive in the military is actually more money than was being spent for food by the average young American. After we deduct the cost of food, we find your civilian peers are left with $1,142 per month to fund their lifestyle.

At this point, we must note the value of the comprehensive healthcare provided by the military. As a service member, comprehensive healthcare is provided, at ***no cost*** to the service member. The average young American spent $1,317 (3.1% of their income) on healthcare in 2023.[51] If we deduct the cost of healthcare ($105 a month), we find that after paying taxes, housing, food and healthcare costs, the average young American has $1037 per month to cover all other expenses.

The $1,860 in disposable income provided to the E-1 in the military is $822 more than the disposable income of their friends outside the military. Indeed, the new service member *–the lowest paid person in the military– has 50% more disposable than their civilian counterparts*. Remember also that the numbers here reflect the service member also paying for half a million dollars in life insurance, compared to a civilian who is choosing not to pay for life insurance.

So, you can live the same lifestyle as your civilian peers and still have more than $800 extra every month. How much of that should be used for investing. Your minimum starting point needs to be the amount that the government will match. As stated earlier in this book, when you contribute to the TSP the government will also put money into your TSP account. You are, in essence giving yourself a pay raise. As of 2025, the government will match the first three percent of your pay that you put into the TSP, dollar for dollar (a 100% match), for the next two percent of your base pay that you contribute, the government provides a 50% match (they contribute 50 cents for every $1.00 you put into the TSP). Although the government does not provide any TSP matching funds during your first two months of service (essentially the time you spend in basic training), and only one percent from that point until after you have served two years, this is still a valuable benefit. From the start, *it is essential that you contribute at least five percent of your base pay* ($107.20) to TSP every month – this is the amount that earns you the maximum matching funds from the government. Not contributing at least five percent is equivalent to choosing to take a pay cut every month. However, you can –and should– contribute even more.

We have already seen that you are making $822 more than your civilian counterparts; this money should be used to build your wealth and create financial independence. Before you put all of that money into your TSP, another monthly expense we need to consider is your "Emergency Fund."

Emergency Fund. Your investments need to stay invested. You should never take money from your retirement accounts until you are retired. Unfortunately, sometimes life gets in the way of our plans; to help cope with the bumps in the road –and avoid having to tap into your investments– you need to build an emergency fund.

Establish a savings account where you can easily access the money on short notice. Never lose sight of the fact that this emergency fund is for emergencies. Emergencies involve health, safety, and protecting your ability to earn an income. Paying the co-pay for your daughter who had to make a visit to an "out-of-network" healthcare provider while on vacation is an emergency. Replacing the transmission in the car that takes you to work is an emergency. Buying a bigger TV is not an emergency. You will put $25 every month into your emergency fund.

Even as an E-1, you are earning enough to put $797 into your TSP every month, even after paying for $500,000 in life insurance coverage and also making a $25 contribution to your emergency fund every month. Even after investing almost $800 in your retirement account, paying for your SGLI coverage and contributing to your emergency fund, you still have the same $1037 per month that your civilian peers have to spend each month (after paying for food, housing and medical care). When you make this investment, you will be starting your path to financial freedom with more than $12,000 (including the government's contributions) being invested in your retirement accounts during your first year in the military.

Because the dollar amounts will change (increase) every year as military pay rises to keep pace with inflation, a percentage of income will probably be more useful to anyone reading this book after 2025. With a base pay of $2,144 and a TSP contribution of $797, the new E-1 is contributing 37% of their base pay to the TSP. The bottom line is that you, ***an E-1 in the military, can contribute hundreds of dollars to your TSP every month and still maintain the same standard of living as your non-military counterparts***. From the first day you are in the military, you can start building wealth in your retirement savings. Your decision to serve in the military means there is no real barrier between you and financial independence!

When you get your first pay raise –which *will* happen four months after you begin your career in the military– you will be making another $175 every month. This could all be added to your TSP contributions (increasing your contributions to 40% of your basic pay), but the reality is that you are probably too busy with training requirements at the three month point in your career to make any changes to your TSP contributions (remember, you need to make the changes a month before you want them to take effect). Therefore, we will assume that you leave your TSP contributions fixed at 37% of your base pay until you are preparing for promotion to E-2. In the first six months of your military career –before you have even earned your first promotion– you will have accumulated $5,000 in your TSP account; you also have $150 in your emergency fund. After six months in the military, you will be promoted to the pay grade of E-2 and will need to recalculate your contributions based on your new pay grade (as discussed in the next chapter).

CHAPTER 8

Putting the Plan into Action: E-2 through E-5

Before your first year in the military is over, you will be promoted to E-2, and your pay (in 2025) will increase to $2,599 every month, a pay raise of $280 each month.

E-2 (Months 6 through 12)

<u>As an E-2</u>
Your starting point: $ 4,957 in your TSP investments
$ 150 in your Emergency Fund
Your actions:
Increase TSP contributions to 45% of your Basic Pay

Your ending point: $12,404 in your TSP investments
$ 300 in your Emergency Fund

Unsurprisingly, little has changed in your financial life in the last six month. Your standard of living hasn't changed. Your expenses haven't changed, your peer group hasn't changed. You are still spending as much as the average American between the ages of 20 and 24 (but saving a lot more). The only thing that has changed after six months in the military is the fact that you are getting paid more. Your current TSP contributions, which you started on "day one" in the military, are still based on your income as an E-1 with less than four months of service. We didn't increase your TSP contributions when you got you "longevity pay increase" for going over four months of service, but now that you are actually getting promoted, we need to adjust your contributions. Because nothing in your life has changed (except the extra income) all of the extra money from your promotion can – and should – be invested in the TSP. Note that, although your pay went up by over $280 when you were promoted, your current basic pay is $455 a month more than you were earning as an E-1 with less than four months of service (Remember, you did not increase your TSP contributions when you went over four month of service).

You might think that you could increase your monthly TSP contributions by the full $455; however, you are only going to be increasing your TSP contribution by $362 – we need to set aside $90 to pay the increased taxes you will now owe. To calculate the increase in tax burden, simply multiply the pay raise by your income tax bracket and then calculate what you will owe for Social Security and Medical taxes due to the pay raise. Under the current tax laws, after promotion to E-2 you move from the 10% tax bracket to the 12% tax bracket (after promotion to E-7 you will move into the 22% tax bracket). So, you need to multiple your pay raise by 12% to determine how much additional income tax you will owe ($455 x 12% = $55). This will actually result in you keeping more money in your bank account than necessary because some of the $455 pay increase will still be taxed at the 10% rate, but keeping back the full 12% makes your math easier. Do the same calculations for the 6.2% for Social Security tax and the 1.45% for Medicare tax ($455 x 6.2% = $28; $455 x 1.45% = $7). **As an E-2, you should be contributing a total of $1,164 (45% of your base pay) to the TSP.** In addition to your contribution, the government is adding another $26 every month. That's now more than $14,000 per year going into your retirement savings!

You will likely be promoted again around the time you have one year in service, but before we look at your situation as an E-3, we're going to look at the wealth you have built during your first year in the military. You and the government partnered to contribute $819 every month as an E-1 (total E-1 contributions = $4,870). As an E-2, you contributed $1,164 a month, with the government adding another $26 every month (total E-2 contributions = $7,112). Simply adding the contributions made by you and the government to this point in your career, we come up with a total of $11,982! That's great, but you'll find your TSP balance is likely even bigger than that. Assuming the L Fund you invested in has returned the 8.35% per year discussed earlier, your balance will be about $12,434. Where did the extra $450 come from? Through the magic of "compounding," your money has begun to work for you – you are no longer the only one earning money! The money that you have in the TSP is earning money just by being invested in the TSP.

Let's return to your impending promotion to E-3 now. You need to change your TSP contributions to 47% of basic pay now. Remember, you need to ***make these changes before you get promoted*** so that they will take effect when you are promoted. For example, if you will be getting promoted to E-3 on June 1st, you need to change your TSP contributions in early May (or even late April). If you wait until late May, you probably won't see your contributions increase until July. It takes time for the finance system to process these changes, so you need to stay ahead of this.

E-3 (1 Year to 2 Years)

As an E-3

Your starting point: $12,404 in your TSP investments
$ 300 in your Emergency Fund

Your actions:

Increase TSP contributions to 47% of your Basic Pay

Your ending point: $29,500 in your TSP investments
$ 600 in your Emergency Fund

One year in and you already have well over $10,000 of wealth accumulated! We aren't going to include the $300 you have in your emergency fund as part of your "wealth"; that money is intended to be spent when an emergency arises, so it is not part of your retirement nest egg. You've now seen that you can live the same lifestyle as the average American and still grow wealth. At this point you are a committed saver.

You've just been promoted to E-3, congratulations. As with the promotion to E-2, it is unlikely that your financial life has changed, other than the fact that you got another pay raise. We add that pay increase ($134, but only $108 increase after taxes) to your TSP contribution. This allows you to **push your monthly TSP contribution to $1,272 (47% of your basic pay)**. The government match will increase to $27.33. During the twelve months that you are an E-3, you and the government will have added a combined total of almost $15,000 to your TSP. Assuming you are not promoted early and spend a full year in the grade of E-3, you finish your second year in the military with a TSP balance of more than $25,000! Yes, your wealth grew more than $15,000 in one year – you are already beginning to pick up speed! Now get ready for promotion to E-4 by increasing your TSP contributions to 51% of basic pay.

E-4 (2 Years to 5 Years)

<u>As an E-4</u>

Your starting point: $ 29,500 in your TSP investments
$ 600 in your Emergency Fund

Your actions:

Increase TSP contributions to 51% of your Basic Pay
Increase TSP to 53% when you go over 3 years

Your ending point: $116,000 in your TSP investments
$ 1,500 in your Emergency Fund

When you make E-4 – about the time you finish your second year in the military – your pay will increase to $3,182. You are now an E-4 with over 2 years of service, so your pay increases due to your promotion, and it also increases due to you getting a "longevity increase" because of your length of service. Longevity increases occur after two years in the military, after three years in the military, after four years in the military and every two years thereafter. The $449 pay raise allows you to **increase your monthly TSP contribution** by $361, after accounting for taxes. This brings your total monthly contributions **to $1,633 (51% of base pay)**.

You will notice that the government is giving you an additional promotion present. Now that you have more than two years of service, the government will increase the amount they are contributing to your TSP account from one percent of your basic pay to five percent of your basic pay. The additional four percent are "matching contributions". Because you were already contributing more than 5% of your pay as an E-4, that same contribution is still more than 5% of E-5 pay, so the government match will increase from 1% of E-3 pay ($27.33) to 5% of E-4 pay ($159.11) – the government gave you an additional $130 pay raise that your teammates who are not investing in the TSP will not be getting because they aren't as committed to achieving financial independence as you are.

At the end of your third year in uniform your TSP balance has almost doubled from last year, now equaling over $54,500. Yes, your TSP balance increased almost much this year as the last two years combined. The pile of money you are building will continue to amaze you as you see how having money actually makes you money. Looking at the $25,000 of growth this year, we see that you contributed $19,592 the government added $1,909, and "the power of compounding" (your money working for you) added more than $3,000. Now that your money is adding thousands of dollars a year to your account, the hundreds of dollars in growth during your first year actually seems small.

Imagine how much more the "power of compounding" will be doing for you in just a few years!

You have now completed three years in uniform and are starting on your fourth year. You may spend this year in the same pay grade, or you might get promoted to E-5. In either case the military has a built-in pay raise for you due to longevity. As an E-4 with more than three years of service, your pay now increases to $3,354.90. This represents a monthly increase of $173; so this money ($139 after taxes) can be added to your monthly TSP, **bringing your total monthly contribution to $1,772 (53% of base pay)**. The government contribution now bumps up to $167.75. At the end of your fourth year, your TSP account has now achieved a total value of more than $80,000.

Your next year unfolds much like that last, you now have four years behind you, and that results in another longevity pay increase. You are now an "E-4 over 4," with a base pay of $3,524.30 ($3,000.40 after taxes). This allows you to add another $136 to your TSP every month, **bringing your total monthly contribution to $1,908 (54% of base pay)**. The government contribution also bumps up to $176.24. During your fifth year of service, your TSP account balance will grow by over $30,000 and break the $100,000 barrier. About $97,000 of your TSP balance is from contributions (from both you and the government), but almost $19,000 of the money in your TSP is just from your money earning money.

E-5 (5 Years to 9.5 Years)

<u>As an E-5</u>

Your starting point: $116,000 in your TSP investments
$ 1,500 in your Emergency Fund

Your actions:

Increase TSP to 56% of Basic Pay upon making E-5
Decrease TSP to 44% when you reach the age of 25
Increase TSP to 46% when you go over 8 years

Your ending point: $306,000 in your TSP investments
$ 2,875 in your Emergency Fund

Year Five. You're older. You're wiser. You're a noncommissioned officer or petty officer now, and you're the person telling the young service members that they really can get wealthy in the military, but they don't believe you when you tell them you have "over $100K in the bank!" Most of them won't believe you, some will ask you "How?!" Tell them! This kind of mentoring is now part of your leadership responsibilities – helping younger service members achieve the same success you are enjoying. As you become an E-5, not much in your day-to-day financial life has changed. The biggest financial adjustments you've had to make are deciding what to do with each pay increase you have received. You have saved prudently and invested wisely; now you have a healthy net worth that you can take pride in. For now, you will again just need to adjust the amount you are investing. When you pinned-on E-5, your basic pay increased from $3,524 to $3,802 a month, an increase of $278. As always, you'll need to account for the increased taxes you'll owe on the higher income. You are in the 12% income tax bracket, so you'll pay an additional $33 in income taxes every month ($278 x 12% = $33.36). You will also be paying more into Social Security and Medicare ($278 x 7.65% = $21.27). After subtracting these taxes from your $278 raise, you would see an increase of just over $223 deposited in your bank account.

All of this can be added to your TSP. This will **bring your monthly TSP deposits to $2,131 (56% of your basic pay)**.

Year Six. Turning 25. Congratulations! When you turned 18, you became old enough to vote; at 21, you became old enough to buy alcohol; now you are old enough to rent a car! You have passed the last hurdle to becoming a "grown up" in our society! This also means you have moved out of the younger demographic and into the "25- to 34-year-old" group. As a consequence, we need to re-evaluate your income and spending to make sure you are still aligned with the lifestyle of your new peer group. The income for this group averages $1,136 a week ($4,923 a month). Looking at their housing expenses, we find that your new peers spend an average of $1,714 a month for housing. They also spend $625 a month on food and just over $219 a month on healthcare. Subtracting these three expenses from their monthly gross income, we find that they have $2,365 (before taxes) to pay for all of their other expenses.[52].[50] After taxes, your civilian peers have $1,548 left every month to cover all other expenses.

Comparing your disposable income to that of your civilian peers, we will see that the $1,548 they have left to spend every month is still less than the $3,295 in disposable income you will have as a 25-year-old E-5 with more than six years of service. Your basic pay has gone up to $3,959.40 because of the longevity pay raise you just received for going over six years of service; after taxes you now have $3,351 to spend every month. Subtracting the $30 for SGLI, $1 for the Armed Forces Retirement Home, and $25 for your emergency fund leaves you with $3,295. However, your TSP contributions have been $2,131 (56% of your basic pay). Continuing your contributions at this level would bring your disposable income down to $1,164 – less than the $1,548 your civilian peers are spending – so we now need to reduce your TSP contributions to ensure you continue to have the same standard of living as your civilian peers. To ensure you have the same disposable income as a civilian, you will now ***reduce*** **your monthly TSP contributions from $2,131 to $1,747 (44% of your basic pay)**; this will give you an additional

$510 more to spend each month than you had as a 24 year-old. If you find your current standard of living acceptable and you don't *need* the extra $510 every month, you can choose to save more aggressively than the model in this book calls for. Remember: every extra dollar you invest now will become a pile of money in the future. In this case, if you keep your contributions the same for just one month, you will have **an extra $6,750 in your TSP when you begin taking withdrawals at the age of 59½**! That extra $6,750 in retirement is from just keeping your TSP contributions at the same level for one month, if you keep your contributions at $2,131 for the entire year, you would have more than $75,000 extra in your TSP account at in retirement (at the age of 59½). Obviously, you can choose to set your TSP contribution somewhere between these two level (for example, giving yourself an extra $150 a month rather than the full $510), this book will assume that you have reduced your contributions to the level that ensures you continue to have the same level of disposable income as your civilian peers.

Years Seven and Eight. Continue. Your pay doesn't change when you pass the seven-year mark of your military career, so there is nothing to be done. You now have well over $175,000 in your TSP so you just need to keep doing what you are already doing.

Years Nine and Ten. Starting your ninth year of service, you get another longevity pay raise as you become an "E-5 over eight." This increases your base pay to $4,142.40, an increase of $183 a month ($147 after taxes). **We add that $147 to your monthly TSP contributions, bringing your monthly contributions to $1,894 (46% of base pay)** each month. The government contribution has also increased to $207 each month. In your ninth year in the military, there are no significant changes so there is nothing for you to do. As you complete your ninth year of service, your TSP balance now stands at just over $280,000 (more than a quarter of a million dollars!). When you start your tenth year of service, you are likely preparing for promotion to E-6. The next chapter will deal with you actions to take after that promotion occurs, but for now, just keep doing what you have been doing.

At this point, it's worth revisiting your Emergency Fund. In 9 years, you have contributed a total of $2,700 to the fund. You have probably spent some of that on emergencies; that's what it's for after all. If you haven't, that's great. As this fund grows, don't be tempted to dip into it for those "lesser emergencies" (like a bigger TV). It's tempting, but you want to build this fund to at least one month's pay built up. Adding $25 a month –and never spending anything–it will take you twenty years to build one month salary in your emergency fund (due in part to the fact that you monthly salary grows almost as fast as your emergency fund). Emergencies tend to get more expensive as you progress through life and you'll be glad to have the money in your emergency fund when you *truly* need it!

CHAPTER 9

Putting the Plan into Action: E-6 and Higher

E-6 (9.5 Years to 15 Years)

<u>As an E-6</u>

Your starting point: **$307,000 in your TSP investments**
$ 2,875 in your Emergency Fund

Your actions:

Decrease TSP to 42% of Basic Pay upon marriage
Increase TSP to 43% when you go over ten years
Decrease TSP to 23% when your first child is born
Invest 100% of your Continuation Pay in an IRA
Increase TSP to 29% when you go over twelve years
Increase TSP to 30% when you go over fourteen

Your ending point: **$625,000 in your TSP investments**
$ 4,500 in your Emergency Fund

You are now finishing your tenth year of service. You are also halfway to being able to retire and receive a military pension. Your TSP balance has also surpassed $300,000! Promotion to E-6 increases your pay by $302. After accounting for income tax, Social Security and Medicare, you will be left with an additional $242 you could add to your TSP every month (increasing your monthly TSP contributions to $2,136, but wait. . . .

Marriage. Changes that you may be considering, or experiencing, include marriage, children and other family-related changes to your circumstance. These changes tend to be welcome, gratifying and just generally good, but all of them tend to cost money.

Because the average American woman gets married at 28.6 years of age (the average man getting married at the age of 30.5), we assume you will be making that transition right around the time you are promoted to the paygrade of E-6.[53] Hence, we now need to revisit some of our assumptions. First, the good news. A newly married service member being promoted to E-6 will find that being able to file their taxes as "married filing jointly" will reduce the amount of income tax they must pay every month as the new filing status doubles the standard deduction that reduces your taxable income. Even though your pay went up, the amount of income tax you need to pay (have withheld from your pay) every month will *decrease* from $328 to $214; effectively increasing your pay by another $114 a month.

Unsurprisingly, the average income for a two-person household in the United States is larger than the average one-person household. Adding a second adult to the home usually means adding a second income. In keeping with the general assumption that your life is similar to the "average" American, we will assume that your spouse makes the same as the average American. Our new comparison group is a two-person household. In 2023, the average annual income for two-person households in the United States was $117,296.[54] Looking at income by education level, rather than household size, reveals that the average American with some college education, or an associates degree, earned $1,089 a week (or $56,628 a year) in 2024.[54] If we double this amount, we find the average American couple with some college education has a household income of $113,256 a year. The fact that the average two-person household has a total income higher than twice the median income for the average American with an associates degree, shows that the average is being skewed upwards by the inclusion of two-person households with bachelors, masters, doctorates, or professional degrees.

Nonetheless, the model here will use the higher income level ($117,296 a year, or $9,774.67 a month) for our civilian comparison group. We will also assume that your new spouse earns the same as the average American with only a high school diploma, adding $930 a week ($4,030 a month) to your household income. So you, as a new E-6 with 9½ years of service earn basic pay of $4,443.90, adding your spouse's income brings your total household income to $8,473,90 a month. Subtracting federal income tax for you and your spouse ($677), Social Security ($525), Medicare ($123), the Armed Forces Retirement Home ($1), SGLI ($30), and your emergency fund ($25), you are left with $7,093 in disposable income every month.

Now for the bad news. We need to make some adjustments to our spending assumptions. We began by comparing your disposable income to the average for Americans between the ages of 20 and 24; we have already changed our benchmark to Americans aged 25 to 34; now we need to look specifically at how families spend their money. Among two-person households in the United States, the average spending on housing was $2,275.50; they also spend $836.67 on food, and $322.42 on healthcare.[55] After marriage, our civilian counterparts have increased their spending on housing by $562 a month and spending on food by $212 a month. They also increased spending on healthcare by $103 a month, but your only health-related change of expenses will be the dental insurance premiums that you will need to pay for your spouse's dental coverage. Beginning with the $9,775 monthly income in the average two-person household, we subtract $833 for income taxes, $606 for Social Security, $142 for Medicare, $2,276 for housing, $837 for food and $322 for healthcare. This leaves our civilian couple with $4,759 in disposable income every month. The increased expenses are more than offset by the increased income in a two-person household, resulting in a net *increase* in disposable income.

Turning to your finances, as a married service member, you will no longer receive meals "in kind"; instead, the government will give you money to purchase your own meals. Your Basic Allowance for Subsistence (BAS) of $465.77 a month, covered *your* meals, but a family of two spends an average of $836.67 on food every month. To determine your added food cost, we subtract your BAS from the $836.67, showing that the average cost of food for a two-person household is $370.90 greater than your BAS. We therefore need to subtract this cost from the disposable income we previously calculated ($7,093 - $371 = $6,722).

Our civilian newlyweds are now spending an additional $103 every month on healthcare. As an active-duty member of the military, your family will receive healthcare with no premiums; however, we assume your spouse does not receive dental health benefit from their employer, so you will need to purchase insurance to cover the dental expenses of your spouse. Your civilian counterparts had healthcare spending go up over $100 a month; your healthcare spending will only go up $12.10 to purchase the dental insurance offered to military family members. This reduces your disposable income to $6,710 a month.

Finally, we assume that you and your spouse are unable to get on-post housing and will be required to live off-base. Living "on base" (receiving housing "in kind") obviously leaves you with no housing bills because the military simply gives you a place to live, but living off base is different. Using the national averages, we will further reduce the amount available for TSP contributions (your disposable income) by the $106 needed to cover housing costs not met by BAH (using the calculations shown in the "Assumptions" chapter). After accounting for increased housing and food costs, your dental insurance premium and realizing the benefit of premium-free healthcare, we see that your disposable income every month is $6,603. This is $1,844 more than your civilian contemporaries – which is great! However, the extra $1,844 is less than the $1,894 you were contributing to the TSP as a single E-5; therefore, you will need to ***reduce the percentage*** **of your pay you contribute to TSP each month (decreasing from 46% of your basic pay to 42%).**

Your tenth in uniform has been a big year. It's no longer just you. You now have a family to share your life with; you're also an E-6, a real leader. By the time you complete ten years of service, your TSP account will have grown to more than $300,000 –well over a quarter of a million–this is a big deal!

Year Eleven. After you complete your tenth year of service, you will get another pay increase. As an E-6 with more than ten years of service, your pay will increase $141.30. a month (from $4,443.90 to $4,585.20. This means you can **increase your TSP contributions by $114 to a total of $1,958 (43% of your basic pay). This is the maximum amount, by law, that you can contribute to your TSP accounts** ($23,500 a year, or $1,958.33 a month).

Near the end of your tenth year of service, or early in your eleventh year of service, something magical is going to happen in your TSP account. You've been working hard to build your TSP balance. The government has also been helping to build your TSP balance. Your money has also been working for you. Of the three factors helping to build your wealth, you've been doing the heavy lifting up to this point, but your TSP is getting ready to overpower you! You noticed a few years ago that your TSP account was adding more to your wealth every month that you ever did. Now, the monthly growth in your wealth should edge above $1,958. This is more than the government allows you to add to the account every month. **Your TSP account is now adding more money to itself than you are allowed to!** This is a great thing, but don't let yourself think "my contributions don't matter anymore." Your contributions continue to be important, they're simply not the biggest contributor to increasing your wealth every month. If you want to grow your wealth even more, you can now explore funding an Individual Retirement Account (IRA). In 2025, you can put up to $7,000 ($583.33 a month) into an IRA for you and up to $7,000 in an IRA for your spouse.

Continuation Pay. Now is the time to revisit the idea of Continuation Pay. You'll recall that this is paid to everyone who agrees to continue to serve until retirement. You will be offered this opportunity between eight and twelve years of service. We assume you receive your Continuation Pay after 10 years of service (the middle of the eligibility window), while serving in the paygrade of E-6.

When you went over ten years of service, your monthly basic pay rose to $4,585.20. Your Continuation Pay will be 2.5 times your base bay (all uniformed services –except the Marine Corps– pay Continuation Pay using a 2.5 multiplier; the Marine Corps uses a 5.0 multiplier, so Marines receive twice as much money for their Continuation Pay bonus). This equals a Continuation Pay incentive of $11,463. Marines receive $22,926, twice as much, because their multiplier is twice as big.

Continuation Pay has income tax withheld. The government sends 22% of your Continuation Pay to the Internal Revenue Service for income tax; this does not mean that you are taxed at the 22% rate, it simply means that 22% of the pay was withheld. If you are married, you will get some of this back as a tax refund, but if you are single, you probably will not. The income tax implications of your Continuation Pay are different if you are single or have a spouse with a high income. In 2025, the 12% tax bracket applies to single taxpayers with taxable incomes between $11,926 and $48,475. As an E-6 with more than eight years of service, your annual basic pay will be $53,327. Being single, your taxable income would be $38,327 (after subtracting the $15,000 standard deduction). With a Continuation Pay incentive of $11,463, your taxable income now totals $49,470 – putting you in the 22% tax bracket – causing you to pay more in taxes this year. To avoid this, simply open a "traditional" IRA and contribute at least $1,000 to it (bringing your taxable income below the $48,475 threshold for the 22% tax bracket). A "traditional" IRA removes the money contributed from your taxable income; if you contribute $1,000 to a traditional IRA, your taxable income would be reduced to $48,470 (below the $48,476 threshold for the 22% tax bracket). You will, of course, be required to pay taxes on the money in your traditional IRA when you withdraw it, but it is unlikely that you will be in the 22% tax bracket when are retired. For married people filing a joint return, the 12% tax bracket applies to those with a taxable income between $23,851 to $96,950. Given that married people also receive a larger standard deduction ($30,000 versus $15,000), a married couple could make up to $126,950 and still be in the 12% tax bracket. When a married service member receives a Continuation Pay incentive of $11,463, the government will withhold 22% of this ($2,521.86), but they would get more than $1,000 of this back in their income tax refund that year because the Continuation Pay had more tax withheld than was necessary. That said, a married Marine could be pushed into the 22% tax bracket if their spouse earns more than $50,697 the year that they receive their Continuation Pay, pushing your combined income over $126,950. The same would be true for other service members whose spouses earned more than $62,160 this year. If your spouse's income puts you in the 22% tax bracket, then the 22% that was withheld from your Continuation Pay will just cover the extra income taxes due. After taxes are withheld, you will receive $8,941 in Continuation Pay ($17,882.28 for a Marine).

What to do with your Continuation Pay is not as simply as sending it to your TSP. If you receive the Continuation Pay after just eight years of service (in your ninth year of service), the model in this book has you contributing $1,590 each month to your TSP account ($19,080 for the year). Adding your Continuation Pay would bring your total TSP Contributions for the year to $29,177. Unfortunately, this is above the $23,500 maximum contribution limit for a 401(k) plan (which includes the TSP). If you have followed this plan–contributing $1,590 each month this year to your TSP account–you can only add another $4,420 to your TSP. After putting $4,420 into your TSP to bring your contributions to the maximum allowable level, you will still have $4,521 of your Continuation Pay left. As mentioned in the discussion of taxes above, this money should also be used to open an IRA, but this time, a "Roth" IRA will likely be a better alternative than a "traditional" IRA. As a Marine, you could get $17,882.28 (after taxes) for continuation pay. Contributing $4,420 to your TSP leaves you another $13,462.28 to invest somewhere else. If you invest that $13,462 in a Roth IRA and let it sit until you are 59½ and can make withdrawals free from any taxes or penalties, it could potentially grow to more than $115,000. The $4,521 available to service members in the other services could grow to almost $40,000 over time (assuming the money is invested in an IRA earning returns approximately equal to the historical average of the S&P500, adjusted for inflation (7%). The beauty of a Roth retirement vehicle (either TSP or IRA) is that all withdrawals are tax free in retirement.

Year Twelve. We will assume that **your first child is born** about one year after you got married. Because your family has grown to include three people, we need to change your comparison group again. Three-person households in the United States actually have a lower income than two-person households (presumably because one parent is working fewer hours outside the home –or not at all– after a child is added to the family). The $9,775 monthly income in the average two-person household is replaced with an average monthly income of $8,384.33 in a three-person household. Given the lower average income, it is not surprising to find that three-person households have lower spending overall than two-person households. The reduced spending is reflected in facts such as the distribution of how their food money is spent. Two-person households spend an average of $863 to eat every month. Three-person households only spend $784 a month on food, but they spend 62.4% of their food budget on meals at home. Conversely, the two-person household spends most of their food budget (50.4%) on meals eaten outside of the home. Three-person households also spend 7% less on housing every month than two-person households; even though the three-person household spends 24% more on utilities than a two-person household.[58] Beginning with the $8,384 monthly income in the average three-person household, we subtract $667 for income taxes, $520 for Social Security, $122 for Medicare, $2,133 for housing, $785 for food and $363 for healthcare. This leaves the average civilian couple with $3,795 in disposable income every month. . . before accounting for childcare costs.

We will assume that your spouse exits the workforce after the birth of your first child. This obviously reduces your household income (we assumed spousal income to be $4,030 a month). With you as the sole breadwinner, your disposable income now breaks down like this: Basic pay is $4,585 a month (E-6, over 10), minus income taxes of $211, Social Security tax of $284 and Medicare taxes of $66, you are left with $4,024 each month. We must also deduct the cost of food that is not covered by your BAH ($319), the 5% "plus up" for BAH ($106), spousal dental insurance ($12.10), the Armed Forces Retirement Home ($1), SGLI ($30) and your emergency fund contributions. This leaves you with $3,531 in disposable income every month. Comparing that to our civilian three-person household, we find they have $3,795 in disposable income every month after accounting for taxes, housing, food and healthcare. However, with a new baby in the family, we need to consider the costs of childcare. The average three-person household in the U.S. includes two wage-earners, although working fewer hours than before the child enters the family. As was discussed earlier, childcare in the United States costs an average of $16,000 a year.[59] That works out to $1,333 a month. Deducting that from our civilian's disposable income, we find they are left with $2,462. This is $1,069 less disposable income than you have in the military (with a spouse *not* working outside the home). So, the birth of your first child will require you to ***reduce*** **your $1,958 TSP contributions by $889 to $1,069 a month (23% of your basic pay)**. Obviously, if your spouse continues to work outside the home, any income in excess of childcare costs could also be used to increase your TSP contributions back up toward the monthly maximum of $1,958.

Years Thirteen and Fourteen. The average American family has two children (technically, the average is 1.94 per family).[60] So we assume that you will have **a second child, born one year after their older sibling**. Your first child now has teeth, so you will want to upgrade your family dental coverage from a single person (your spouse) to a family plan that will also cover your children. This will increase your dental premiums from $12.10 to $31.46 a month. This higher premium will cover your spouse and all the children you may have. The average American family with four people has essentially the same income as a three-person household (99.5%). Their expenses are roughly the same, with the exception of food. Here we find the that the four-person household spends an average of $80 a month more for food than the four-person household.[61] The average four-person household has an average monthly income of $8,339. Four-person households in the United States spend an average of $865 a month on food, $2,248 on housing and $346 for healthcare every month.[62] Beginning with the $8,339 monthly income in the average three-person household, we subtract $661 for income taxes, $517 for Social Security, $121 for Medicare, $2,248 for housing, $865 for food, $346 for healthcare, and $1,333 for childcare costs. This shows us that the average civilian couple with two children has $2,247 in disposable income every month.

You will receive a pay increase now that you have completed 12 years of service, taking your basic pay from $4,585,20 to $4,858.80 (an increase of $273.60). When we subtract the increased income taxes ($32.84) and increased Medicare and Social Security payments ($20.93 combined), you are left with an increase of $219.83. We now need to account for the increases in spending for food ($80) and dental insurance (increase from $12.10 to $31.46 = $19.36). Subtracting these expenses from the $219.83 pay increase leaves an additional $120.47 that can be added to your TSP every month. You can now **increase your TSP contributions to $1,404 (29% of your basic pay).** Once you update your TSP contributions, you can leave everything on "cruise control" for the next two years (until you go over 14 years of service).

Year Fifteen. When you complete 14 years of service, your basic pay will increase from $4,858.80 to $4,942.50 (an increase of $83.70). After taxes, Medicare and Social Security, you are left with $67.25. This should be used to **increase your TSP contributions to $1,471 (30% of your basic pay).**

E-7 (15 to 24 Years)

<u>As an E-7</u>
Your starting point: $ 625,000 in your TSP investments
$ 4,500 in your Emergency Fund
Your actions:
Increase TSP to 35% of Basic Pay upon making E-7
Decrease TSP to 5% when you turn 35 years-old

Your ending point: $1,450,000 in your TSP investments
$ 7,200 in your Emergency Fund

You are now a senior noncommissioned officer or chief petty officer, and your TSP balance recently passed through the half a million dollars point! Remember when $50,000 seemed like a lot of money?

When you were promoted to E-7 (at 15 years of service), your basic pay rose to $5,621 form the previous $4,942.50 (as an E-6 over 14). This leaves you with an extra $545 (after taxes) in disposable income every month. Unfortunately, not all of this can be added to your TSP contributions. Remember the maximum amount, by law, that you can contribute to your TSP accounts is $23,500 a year ($1,958.33 a month). You now need to **increase your TSP contributions by $487 to $1,958 (35% of your basic pay).** The extra $58 a month can be added to your emergency fund, or to a Roth IRA.

The final adjustment to our model comes after 16 years of service, when you reach the age of 35. Our civilian comparison group changes to match our age (35- to 44-years of age), and we find that the average yearly income for a four-person household between the ages of 35 and 44 is just under $150,000 ($12,479.58 a month). It must be noted that the median income for the 35- to 44year-old age group is $77,376 per year ($1,488 per week), so the average American four-person household obviously has two income-earners.[63] As their income has increased, so too has their monthly spending: housing ($2,911), food ($1,154) and healthcare ($570). Childcare remains at the national average ($1,333 a month). After these expenses, income taxes, Social Security and Medicare, we find their disposable income is now $4,398 per month.[64]

At this point in life, most people have begun contributing to their retirement (as you have been doing for the last 16 years). Looking at what our civilian peers, we see that they contribute an average of $1,298 every month to Social Security and pension plans. We have already subtracted their $774 in monthly Social Security contributions, so we see they are also contributing an average of $524 to their retirement. Subtracting this from their disposable income, we find they have $3,874 in disposable income.

As an E-7 with 16 years of service, your pay will increase to $5,781.30. We then subtract income tax ($354), Social Security ($358), Medicare ($84), $30 for SGLI, $1 for the Armed Forces Retirement Home, $31.46 for dental insurance, $106 to supplement your BAH, $688 to supplement your BAS and $25 for your emergency fund. This leaves us with $4,103 compared to the civilians' disposable income of $3,874. You now have $229 to contribute to your TSP and maintain the same level of disposable as your civilian counterparts. Remember that we are comparing a military household, with only one income, to the average civilian household with two incomes and finding that they have roughly the same amount of disposable income every month. Because your single-income military household has about the same disposable income as the average American family of the same age and size, we are going to reduce your TSP contributions. You could reduce your TSP contributions to $229, but you should absolutely keep your TSP contributions to at least 5% of your basic pay to ensure you get the full government match for your contributions. Hence, we will reduce your TSP contributions to $289 a month (5% of your basic pay). This is a significant change in your retirement savings. You have gone from contribution the maximum amount allowable last year, to contributing the minimum amount needed to get the full "employer matching funds" from the government. If you don't need to reduce your month contributions by $1,700, you should maintain them at the maximum level; alternatively, you could select some contribution level in the middle ground. Nonetheless, the model presented in this book will assume that you are now contributing only 5% of your basic pay to the TSP (and that your spouse has no income). It is worth noting that maintaining your TSP contributions at 5% of your basic pay ($289 a month) means your disposable income during your 16th and 17th years of service will be $60 a month ***less*** than your civilian peers. However, after you go over 18 years of service, your pay increases by $170 a month; leaving your TSP contributions at 5% will mean that you will have $68 a month ***more*** disposable income than your civilian peers. When you go over 20 years of service, your 5% TSP contributions will now equal $300 a month and you will have an additional $117 a month more disposable income than your civilian peers (that you could add to your TSP if you chose to do so).

Your TSP is now on "cruise control." You're getting the maximum government matching funds, and your pile of money is adding more value to your account every year than you are! Here is the projected balance of your account for the next nine years:

At the end of 16 years: $707,000
17 years: $775,000
18 years: $850,000
19 years: $930,000
20 years: $1,020,000 (You're a millionaire!)
21 years: $1.1 Million
22 years: $1.2 Million
23 years: $1.3 Million
24 years: $1.45 Million

Now for an unpleasant truth. As was mentioned earlier, inflation causes things to cost more in the future than they cost today. Looking at this in the other direction, we can see that a dollar that we have today can buy more things than one dollar will buy in the future. Inflation causes prices to increase, which causes the value of our money to decrease over time.

Because we are now looking decades into the future, we need to calculate the "present value" of our TSP account. If we assume a 3% rate of inflation over the course of the 24-year military career, the $1,458,000 that you have in your TSP then has the same value as $717,000 today. That's still almost a quarter million dollars! If we allow that money to continue to grow until we reach the age of 59½ (when we can withdraw the money without penalty), it will grow to $5.7 million, equivalent to $2,800,000 today (almost three million dollars!)

<u>**E-8? (E-9?)**</u>
E-8 ending point: $1.7 Million in your TSP (26 years)
E-9 ending point: $2.4 Million in your TSP (30 years)
E-9 ending point: $5.9 Million in your TSP (at age 59½)

A select few of you may be promoted beyond E-7, reaching the very highest ranks of the enlisted force; the vast majority of you will not. If you are one of the chosen few who makes E-9 (about 1% of the enlisted force), and you continue to contribute to your TSP until retirement at 30 years, you can look forward to a final balance in excess of $2 million dollars!

How much will you need in retirement? If we look at your active duty pay as an E-9 (over 28), you received $8,928.60 in base pay ($7,514 after taxes) and $465.77 in BAS. You contributed at least $447 to TSP (5%), leaving your take home pay at $7,532 (excluding housing). If we then add our $2,700 "guestimate" for your housing costs; we can estimate that you will need about $10,230 a month ($122,800/year) in retirement to maintain your lifestyle. You've grown to have a very nice lifestyle during your 30-year career!

There is an exception to the requirement to wait until age 59½ to take money out of your TSP/401(k) without penalty: if you leave the military after you turn 55 you can draw money from your TSP immediately. Because you've been in the military for 30 years, you may be over 55 at retirement and, therefore, able to start funding your retirement from your TSP on the day you retire. You can begin taking regular withdrawals from your $2.4 million TSP account immediately and without penalty. We must also remember the $8,941 (after taxes) of Continuation Pay that you contributed to a Roth IRA twenty years ago. Invested in an S&P Index Fund, returning an average of 10% a year, your Continuation Pay will have grown to more than $65,500 over the next 20 years of your career.

In this case, the "present value" (that is, the equivalent value in 2025) of your $2.4 million dollar TSP account and your $65,500 IRA at age 55. The value of these accounts will be just over $1,017,000 in 2025 dollars.[65] If you use the "4 percent" rule of thumb, taking out 4% of your TSP ($40,685 in 2025 dollars) every year in retirement, you'll have an income stream of $3,390 every month. Your withdrawals from your Roth TSP are not subject to taxes; you get to keep it all! Adding your military pension ($6,696; $6,233 after taxes) to your retirement account withdrawals ($3,390) you'll have a total retirement income of just over $9,600 every month ($115,000 a year). Although this income is $650 a month less than your total compensation as a active duty E-9 with thirty years of service, it is substantially more than the average American family earns. You have achieved financial independence –at the age of 55–and you never need to work again! Also remember that your Social Security benefits can begin in as little as seven years. This will bring your total income to a level ***higher*** than you were earning on active duty!

Assuming you joined the military at age 19 and retire at the age of 49 (rather than 55 or older), you will leave your money in the TSP until you turn 59½; by this time your account balance will have grown to about $5.7 million. When we look at the "present value" of that amount, we see that this would be worth about $1.7 million in 2025 dollars. Including your IRA (funded only with your Continuation Pay, and now worth $186,000), your total retirement accounts are worth $1.75 in 2025 dollars. Applying the 4% rule, this will create an income stream of $5,800 every month. Adding your military pension ($6,233 after taxes), brings your total retirement income to just over $12,000 per month, or about $144,000 per year – a very nice retirement indeed!

---

65 Assumes an average rate of inflation of 2.5%, the expected 30-year rate of inflation forecast by the Federal Reserve Bank of St. Louis (https://fred.stlouisfed.org/series/EXPINF30YR)

CHAPTER 10

Financial Planning as you Retire from the Military

As you prepare to transition out of the military, there will be a number of questions that you will ask yourself. The (literal) $10,000 question is: "Should I take terminal leave or sell my leave back to the government?" When you reach the end of your military career, you will probably have a substantial amount of unused leave accrued and you will need to decide if you want to take "terminal leave" or sell your unused leave back to the government. This is a subject of much misinformation, so ensure you know the facts and don't be swayed by the misunderstanding about terminal leave that are very prevalent in the military (even among people with decades of service).

During your career, you will earn 30 days of leave each year. The intent is that you use this leave, and you should. Taking regular leave helps you maintain a healthy family life and is good for your physical and mental well-being as well. Under normal circumstances, the military does not allow you to accrue more than 60 days of leave. This is done to ensure that you do, in fact, take leave on a regular basis. If you have more than 60 days of leave accrued on the 1st of October, anything over 60 days will simply be deleted from your account.

Whenever you reenlist, extend your enlistment, or leave the military, you will have the opportunity to sell your unused leave back to the government. You can sell a maximum of 60 days of leave throughout your entire career. Considering that the amount you are paid when you sell leave back to the government is equal to 1/30th of one month's pay (i.e., one day's pay) per day of leave sold, selling leave later in your career (when your base pay is higher) is going to be more lucrative than selling leave early in your career. For example, if you sell back five days of leave when you reenlist at the end of your first 4-year enlistment, as an E-4 you would be paid $101.66 for each day, for a total of $508.30 for five days of leave. If you were to sell back five days when you retire as an E-7 with 24 years of service, you would be paid $207.94 for each day of leave; a total of $1,039.70 for five days (more than twice as much!). By selling the five days of leave early in your career, you have given up over $500 in potential income. If you sell back the maximum amount of leave (60 days) as at E-7 retiring at 24 years, you will be paid $12,476! This is not an insignificant amount of money.

Here are the two persistent misunderstandings about selling leave back to the government:

Myth: "You pay 25% taxes on any leave you sell back." **No.** It is ***NOT*** taxed at the 25% rate. This misunderstanding comes from the fact that taxes are withheld when you sell leave, and the amount withheld is equal to 25% of the total. What the misinformed don't understand is that taxes *withheld* are different than taxes *paid*. If you sell back leave worth $10,000, you will only see $7,500 in your bank account; the other $2,500 will be sent to the Internal Revenue Service. When you file your taxes at the end of the year, the excess taxes will be returned to you as part of your income tax refund. If you are in the 12% tax bracket, your income tax refund would be increased by $1,300 due to the excess taxes withheld from the sale of your leave. If you are in the 22% tax bracket, the excess of $300 would be returned to you. No one in the military is in the 25% tax bracket (except generals and admirals) so, unless you are an admiral or general, you will ***not*** pay 25% taxes on the leave you sell. Remember, you must see the big picture. A dollar that the government sends in your tax refund is just as good as the dollar the government sends you at the time you sell your leave.

Myth: "You lose money when you sell leave." This misunderstanding results from the fact that you are not paid your housing allowance, subsistence allowance, etc. when you sell leave. Conversely, if you take terminal leave you are paid your full pay and all allowances. This myth is very easy to debunk with a simple example. Two service members with the exact same pay and allowance are retiring on the same day, with the same years of service. They will both retire on April 1st. Soldier One decides to use his 60 days of accrued leave to take terminal leave. Soldier Two decides to sell his 60 days of accrued leave to the government. At the end of January, they both receive exactly the same amount of pay and allowances; to this point in their careers, they have received the exact same amount of pay from the military. On January 31st, Soldier One begins his 60 days of terminal leave. Soldier Two continues his normal duties. At the end of February, they both receive the same pay and allowances. Soldier Two obviously receives his full pay and allowances because he is still working. Soldier One also receives his full pay and allowance, because he is entitled to that while taking leave. At the end of March, both service members again receive their full pay and allowance. This is the last day of both servicemembers' 24-year career, and they have received – to the penny – the exact same pay from the government; the only difference is that Soldier Two still has 60 days of leave to sell back to the government. Soldier Two sells his leave to the government for $12,476; he receives $9,357 immediately and another $1,621 when his tax over-payment is refunded. At the end of their careers the only differences are that the service member who used leave worked 60 days less than the service member who sold leave and the service member who sold leave has received $10,978 more in total pay than the service member who used all of his leave. Bottom line: Both service members are paid exactly the same amount until they day they retire (they both receive full pay and allowances for their entire term of service), but the service member who sells leave ***also*** gets paid an additional 60 days of basic pay (the other Soldier enjoyed a 60-day vacation instead of the $10,000).

Monthly Pay & Leave Balance for Leave-taker and Leave-seller

	Leave-taker	Leave-seller
January:	$8,000 & 60 days leave	$8,000 & 60 days leave
February:	$8,000 & 30 days leave	$8,000 & 60 days leave
March:	$8,000 & 0 days leave	$8,000 & $10,978 (leave sold)
TOTAL:	$24,000	$34,978

The decision to take terminal (retirement) leave involves a lot of variables unique to each individual. Financially speaking, it is always to your advantage to sell leave to the government unless you *must* begin a new job before your retirement date (or lose the job), or if you will be starting a job that pays *more* than your basic pay. If you take terminal leave, you are "leaving money on the table." You will be paid less by the military than your twin who sells leave, but you are accepting this loss in the expectation that you can make up the loss with the income from you new job.

Transitioning from Saver to Spender. You began this journey because you were willing to make a change. You committed yourself to years of saving and investing, and now you are seeing the results of your work, your sacrifice, your patience. Now you need to make a change again. The change from "saver" to "spender" can be more difficult than the change from spender to saver. You now have the "big pile of money" that you set out to create. When you look at your investment statements, you take justifiable pride in what you have done. It can be very hard to deliberately begin to dismantle this impressive thing that you have created. Remember though, that was the whole point of this process. You created this nest egg to ensure a secure retirement; you need to use it for that purpose.

Military Retirement

Under the military's Blended Retirement System (BRS), the government will guarantee you a lifetime income equal to two percent of your income times your number of years of service. Retiring in the pay grade of E-7, after only 20 years of service, the government would provide you a guaranteed pension of over $28,000 a year for life. If you retire from the military at the age of 38, and collect this guaranteed pension for forty years, until you die at the age of 78, the government will have paid you ***over a million dollars after you retired***! Add in the value of the retiree medical benefit ("Tricare for Life") and the Social Security benefit you will earn during your military career, and you will be in *much* better financial shape than most Americans. And remember, this doesn't include the $1,000,000 you have accumulated on your own.

Military Pension. You can now retire from the military after 24 years of service and begin drawing your military pension. With 24 years of service, you will be entitled to 48% (2% for each year of service) of your basic pay (based on the average of your three highest paying years). In 2025, your high-three years of income would average to $6,165; putting your retirement check at $2,959 a month for the rest of your life. That would be $2,913 after taxes – you don't pay Social Security or Medicare taxes on this income, and you have dropped back into the 10% tax bracket (again assuming your spouse has no income). Your retirement check will actually get bigger every year due to annual cost of living increases! The average American aged 45- to 54-years-old earns $1,468 a week ($6,361 a month; $5,451 after taxes, Social Security and Medicare). Your civilian counterparts are also paying an average of $682.25 a month in healthcare costs. As a military retiree, you will want to stay covered by Tricare, the military's health insurance provider. Tricare for retirees has a $900.96 enrollment fee each year (equates to $75.08 a month), and no deductibles.[66] If you are treated in a military treatment facility (yes, retirees can be treated in military hospitals), you pay for nothing except the food you eat! Tricare will save you about $607 every month, relative to your civilian peers. After accounting for healthcare costs, you are only getting paid $1,751 a month less every month than someone your age who is working full time; that works out to about $10 an hour. Unsurprisingly, your military retirement check comes just short of providing you the same standard of living as the average American who is still working full-time. You are, however, now in a position to make choices that most Americans cannot afford.

A Post-military Job? Obviously, the longer you continue to work after you retire from the military, the higher your lifetime income will be, and earning more money is obviously a great way to build even more wealth. But there are additional reasons to consider working after you conclude your time in the military. Continuing your working life after the military means you can allow your investments to grow because you are using the income from your job (and military retired pay) to pay the bills, instead of drawing funds from your retirement accounts. You will also see in the discussion of Social Security, in a subsequent chapter, an example illustrating the value of adding additional years of income to your Social Security earnings (potentially adding more than $300,000 to your lifetime income).

Another factor implicit in much of the discussion above needs to be stated plainly: your employment aspects *after* your military service will be much better than they were before you joined the military. It is a fact that you will leave the military with decades of leadership and managerial experience – regardless of the job you perform in the military. It is highly likely that you will acquire a multitude of marketable skills during your military career. Obviously, different career fields will offer different skills, but all of them will equip you with in-demand skills that will allow you to get a better job than you could have hoped for before you joined the military. It is also highly likely that you will have achieved a higher level of education during your military career. The degree (or degrees) that you earn in the military will also make you a more desirable applicant for almost any job. If you seek employment with the government after you retire from the military, you will receive a veterans' preference in the hiring process; while this doesn't guarantee you a job, it does make you more competitive than a non-veteran applicant with the same skills and experience; this is true for all federal government jobs and many state government jobs as well.

A low-stress post-military job? If you wanted to continue to let your money grow, you could get an entry-level job at just about any business anywhere and bring your income up to the level of your civilian peers; remember the difference in income between your military pension and the average American full-time employee your age is only about $10 an hour. This would allow you to continue to enjoy a lifestyle on par with your non-military peers, while still allowing the retirement savings in your TSP to continue growing.

A high-paying job? If you wanted to maximize your lifetime income, you could use the knowledge, skills and abilities you gained in the military to obtain a good-paying civilian career for your "second act." The average veteran, in every age group, earns more than the average non-veteran. For people in their 40's, the average veteran earns over $11,500 more each year than the average non-veteran.[67] This would allow you to enjoy a more comfortable lifestyle; again allowing the retirement savings in your TSP to continue growing. Another aspect of being retired from the military that can be of cash value is the fact that you already have healthcare covered; you can use this to bargain for higher pay by letting an employer know that you won't need their health insurance coverage (which costs them money to provide). Left to grow until you reach the age of 59½, your TSP could be more than $4.5 Million Dollars (equivalent to $1.4 million in today's dollars)!!!

Just Stop Working? If you never want to work again, you don't have to. Because you contributed to a *Roth* TSP, you can withdraw any contributions you made to the plan, without penalty, after they have been in the account for at least five years. At this point, you have contributed just over $316,000 to your TSP; about $289,000 of your contributions have been in your Roth TSP for more than five years, and it will take you more than five years you spend down that sum, so the remaining contributions will be available to you as well. All of the funds in your TSP (contributions and earnings) will be available to withdraw without penalty once you turn 59½. Simple math suggests that drawing from that $316,000 during the 16½ years (198 months) until you turn 59½ could give you $1,599 a month. Remembering that the average American aged 45- to 54-years-old earns $5,451 (after taxes) every month. Your military pension alone leaves you with $1,751 a month less every month than you civilian peers working full time (after accounting for healthcare costs). Your TSP withdrawals bring that difference down to $152 a month. Now, let's consider the fact that that $1,599 that you are drawing from your Roth TSP account every month is tax free! That means that you don't have to pay income tax, Social Security tax, or Medicare tax on that money; this increases the value of these dollars. If we simply look at the income tax advantage, even if we assume the lowest tax rate (10%), that's essentially $159 extra every month that you save in income taxes. Not paying Social Security saves another $99 and not paying Medicare on your TSP withdrawals saves another $23 every month. In the final analysis, you can quit working when you retire from the military, and still have more disposable income than the average civilian who is still working full time.

With all of that in mind, you may want to also consider the impact that stopping work at the age of 43 will have on your Social Security benefits. Your Social Security pension is based on the money you made during the highest-paying 35 years in your working life. If you retire after 24 years in the military, and do not get a post-military job, the Social Security Administration will base your benefit on the earnings from your 24-year military career and 11 years of zero income. When you retire from the military your monthly income has averaged $4,603 a month over the last 24 years; if you have no other income before claiming social security, adding in 11 zero-income years brings your average monthly earnings down $3,156. Hence your Social Security benefit will be less than 70% of what it might have been if you had continued working for another 11 years after retiring from the military (and leaving the workforce then, at the age of 55, is still a very early retirement).

Full Retirement

Age 59½. . . Really Retire! (Financial Independence). If you decide not to work after you retire from the military, you might have withdrawn your TSP contributions to get you to the age of 59½. In this case, you will have approximately $4.6 million left in your TSP. If you chose *not* to touch your TSP before reaching 59½ you should have about $5.3 million in your TSP. Of this amount, about $66,400 is from government contributions (that's a lot of money, but you'll notice it is now essentially "rounding error" when we are describing your wealth). These government contributions are different, in that the government put pre-tax dollars into a "traditional" plan (the government didn't pay the income tax when they made these contributions). As a result, you will need to pay income taxes on these funds when they are withdrawn, but the other millions of dollars in the account can now be taken out without any penalties or taxes.

When you look at turning your TSP into a lifetime of retirement income, there are two easy alternatives. The TSP will allow you to use the money in your TSP account to purchase an "annuity." This is, in essence, an insurance policy. You pay all of your money up front, and the annuity guarantees to pay you a certain amount for the rest of your life (and your spouse's life). The other option is to simply make your own withdrawals from your TSP account as needed to provide you with a comfortable retirement.

TSP Annuities. If withdrew your contributions before you turned 59½, you still have enough in the account to purchase a TSP annuity that will provide you and your spouse with about $5,600 a month (that's almost a quarter of a million dollars a year!) for the rest of your lives. This amount will also increase by 2% every year to keep pace with inflation. If one of you dies, the other will continue to receive the same amount for the rest of their life. If both of you die before all the money you paid to purchase the annuity has been given back to you, your beneficiaries will receive the difference. If you didn't tap into your TSP before now and have full amount to purchase a TSP annuity, the monthly payment would start at about $6,100 a month (about $73,200 a year). Your monthly payments could be higher if you chose the options to: 1) only get paid during your life so your spouse gets nothing after you die –you also have the option to have your spouse get 50%, 2) not have the payments increase by 2% every year, and 3) not have anything go to your beneficiaries if you die before you get all of your money back. If you chose all of these options, your monthly payment for a $1.4 million TSP annuity would be just over $8,875 a month (about $106,500 a year), *tax-free*!

The beauty of buying an annuity is that it is insurance against running out of money before you run out of life. You are guaranteeing a lifetime of income. The downside of the annuity is that you lose control over your retirement money. You own the annuity, but the TSP now owns the money you spent to purchase the annuity. Because the money is no longer yours, you cannot leave it to you children (or other worthy causes). You can also choose to use only a portion of your TSP to purchase an annuity. If, for example, you use just $500,000 to purchase an annuity, the annuity will still guarantee you and your spouse an income of more than $2,175 a month for life, and you still have almost a million dollars to spend as you see fit. You can explore TSP annuity options online at: https://www.tsp.gov/calculators/tsp-annuity-calculator/#panel-1

Managing Your Own Retirement. You've been an investor for more than a couple decades now; you probably have the financial savvy to manage your own retirement funds. Let's assume you have left your TSP account untouched until you turn 59½ and you have $5.3 million in the account (although we will use the $1.4 million in "2025 dollars" for these calculations). Conventional wisdom says you can withdraw 4%

of your retirement accounts every year, and increase them every year to account for inflation, and have a high probability of the money lasting 30 years or more.[68] With $1.4 million, that would give you an additional income of $57,000 a year. You have a very nice income, and you have complete control over all of your money. When you do die, there will likely be a nice pile of money that you can leave to your heirs and other causes you want to support.

Individual Retirement Accounts. At a couple of points during your career (when you were an E-6 and an E-7), you were contributing the maximum amount allowed by law to your TSP account. After maxing out your monthly TSP contributions you may have had some more "extra money" every month. How can you use this money to further build your wealth? To "supercharge" your wealth building plan you should open an Individual Retirement Account (IRA); this is strongly encouraged but not necessary to reach your $1,000,000 goal. An IRA is much like the TSP, except that it is not managed by your employer. You are responsible for managing this account (that's the "Individual" part of an Individual Retirement Account). A quick internet search will provide you with an endless number of companies that can help you invest your IRA dollars. You can open an IRA for yourself, or for your spouse, or both. Even if your spouse does not have a retirement plan of their own, this is an opportunity to open a "Spousal IRA" for them. If you file a joint tax return, your spouse does not even need to have income for you to contribute to their IRA. You can each contribute up to $7000 a year ($583.33 a month) to an IRA. The United States Congress increases this amount periodically, so if you are at or near the limit make sure you check to see if the limit has increased. There are also higher contribution limits if you are over 50 years of age ("catch up" contributions).

As you enter the final phase of your career, your focus will shift from "how much money do I have?" to "how much money do I need?" Knowing if the pile of money you have created is (or will be) big enough is at least as important as the size of the pile itself. Looking at the projected balance of your account through your retirement at the end of 24 years of service to the nation we can see that you will retire with over $1,400,000 in your TSP account at the age of 59½. You will retire from the military as a millionaire, but there's even better news. Since around the time you made E-6, your money has been contributing more to your TSP than you have. It is growing even more now. Did you notice that even though your TSP contributions were never more than $23,500 a year, your TSP balance is now growing by over $70,000 a year? Your money is doing most of the work now. Just leave this money invested – no more contributions (you can't make contributions to the TSP once you retire)– and your money will continue to grow. The age of 59½ is key because this is when you can withdraw your TSP funds without having to pay a penalty to the Internal Revenue Service.

Because you invested in a Roth fund, you *could* withdraw your *contributions* penalty-free after they have been in the fund for five years, but the *earnings* must stay until you reach the age of 59½. The longer you leave your money invested, the more it will grow; if you *need* to pull out money upon retirement, you have just over $270,000 in contributions that have been in the TSP for five years or longer and can be withdrawn at any time.

The best course of action is to continue working until age 59 ½. The good news is that you can take just about any job and maintain your lifestyle. If we look at your last paycheck as an E-7 with more than 22 years of service, you received $6,238.20 in base pay and $465.77 in BAS. You contributed $1958 to TSP, leaving your take home pay at $4,745.97. This, plus the cost of your housing, should give us a good idea of what you'll need to maintain your lifestyle in retirement. Calculating the cost of housing 24 years in the future at an unknown location is, understandably, impossible. In 2025, the average mortgage payment in the U.S. was about $2,209 per month.[69] If we allow $500 for utilities, we get a $2,700 figure that should be a fair "guestimate" for your housing costs. Hence, we can estimate that you will need about $7,000 a month to maintain your lifestyle. Your military pension will pay you about $3,698 a month for the rest of your life, so you only need to earn another $3,300 a month (about 60% of your base pay as an E-7) until you start to withdraw funds from your TSP at age 59 ½ and truly retire.

Again, when you do reach age 59½, you'll have about $4.8 million in the TSP. That's the good news. Here's the bad news: inflation. Remember the real estate example at the start of the book? You great uncle Steve bought a house for a dime then sold it 90 years later for a million dollars. We then learned that he didn't really make any money. Because of inflation a dollar in the future is worth less than a dollar today. Because we are not actually living 24 years in the future, we need to discount the value of your retirement to understand what it would be worth today. Without going into the math, if we assume a 3% rate of inflation, the value of your $4.8 million at age 59½ (40 years in the future) is worth a little more than $1.3 million today. It's not $5 million, but you are a millionaire.

There is a financial rule of thumb that suggests you can safely withdraw 4% from your retirement accounts and be fairly confident the money will sustain you for at least 30 years. Taking 4% from your TSP balance of $1.3 million ($56,000) each year gives you a monthly retirement income of about $4,650. If we add in your military pension ($2,959) to this, you'll have a total retirement income of $7,609 a month ($91,000 a year). This is well above the $7,000 we estimated you would need, even if our housing estimate was well under your actual needs. Your pile of money is indeed big enough to fund your retirement. It is big enough to allow you to enjoy an even better lifestyle than you did when you were working! You have achieved financial independence!

Social Security

Yes, you will be entitled to a Social Security pension based on your military service. The model in this book assumes that you retire from the military after 24 years of service. We can use this to develop an estimate of your Social Security pension based on your military service.

The amount you receive from Social Security depends on the amount you pay into Social Security. Every year you continue to work (and pay into Social Security), the bigger your pension benefit. As you earn more money, your Social Security taxes will go up, but this will also increase the pension you receive from Social Security. During your military career, you only paid taxes on your basic pay. All of your allowances were tax-free; this means you did not pay Social Security taxes on any of your allowances (for example BAH and BAS), so this are not included in determining your earnings for Social Security benefits.

Your Social Security pension is based on the money you made during the highest paying 35 years in your working life. If you retire after 24 years in the military, and do not get a post-military job, the Social Security Administration will base your benefit on the earnings from your 24-year military career and 11 years of zero income.

Indexing Your Wages. As time goes by, inflation tends to cause wage increases. The Social Security Administration accounts for this by adjusting ("indexing") your wages to account for the fact that a dollar you earned in 2025 will have more value than a dollar you earned in 2049. Think of it this way: if a hamburger cost $1.00 in 2025, it will likely cost much more in the year 2050 (let's say $2.50). To index your earnings, using the notional data from our hamburger example, the Social Security Administration would index you earnings by multiplying your 2025 earnings by 2.5; if you earned one hamburger in 2025, when they calculate the value of those wages in 2050, they will adjust it to be more like to cost of a year 2050 hamburger ($2.50) instead of leaving it at the actual (one hamburger) amount you earned in 2025 (that is, $1.00).

Using the current military pay rates, we can estimate your annual income over the course of your career without the need to estimate the future value of your income. Think of it this way: a retired E-7 leaving the service in 2025 (after 24 years of service) will be earning $74,858 a year. When she first joined the military in 2001, the E-1 paygrade made $964.80 a month ($11,577.60 a year). In 2025, a service member in the E-1 paygrade will make $1949.10 a month ($23,389.20 a year); more than twice as much. We could estimate an indexing factor of about two and double the money she made as an E-1 – and then repeat that process to determine an approximate indexing factor for each year. Looking forward is more complex (and involves more "guessing") as we try to estimate how much inflation will impact wages in the future. Rather than trying to use our crystal ball to determine your future earnings, we can simply use 2025 numbers for all of our calculations. Using "current dollars" for all calculations effectively includes the "indexing" and will simplify our calculations.

Here is your estimated income from a 24-year military career (Remember: You only pay Social Security tax on "base pay"):

Year 1 (Paygrade = E1 & E2): $26,189
Year 2 (Paygrade = E3): $29,815
Year 3 (Paygrade = E4): $34,715
Year 4 (Paygrade = E4): $36,598
Year 5 (Paygrade = E4): $38,452
Year 6 (Paygrade = E5): $42,206
Year 7 (Paygrade = E5): $45,166
Year 8 (Paygrade = E5): $45,166
Year 9 (Paygrade = E5): $48,262
Year 10 (Paygrade = E5 & E6): $50,794
Year 11 (Paygrade = E6): $55,022
Year 12 (Paygrade = E6): $55,022
Year 13 (Paygrade = E6): $58,306
Year 14 (Paygrade = E6): $58,306
Year 15 (Paygrade = E6): $59,310
Year 16 (Paygrade = E7): $67,457
Year 17 (Paygrade = E7): $69,376
Year 18 (Paygrade = E7): $69,376
Year 19 (Paygrade = E7): $71,413
Year 20 (Paygrade = E7): $71,413
Year 21 (Paygrade = E7): $72,205
Year 22 (Paygrade = E7): $72,205
Year 23 (Paygrade = E7): $74,858
Year 24 (Paygrade = E7): $74,858
Years 25 through 35 (Retired): $0.00 (no post-military income)

Total Earnings = $1,326,490. Average of 35 Years' Earnings = $37,900.

Although your average military income over a 24-year career was more than $50,000 a year, when the Social Security Administrations includes the 11 years with no income, the average drops to less than

$40,000 a year. If you continue to work after retiring from the military, your Social Security pension could be much larger.

The Social Security Administration uses "bend points" that reduce the amount of Social Security paid as your income increases. People with lower income have a larger percentage of their income replaced by Social Security than higher earners. In 2025, the bend points are $1,226 and $7,391. Your Social Security pension will replace 90% of the first $1,226 of your average monthly earnings and 32% of your average monthly earnings between $1,226 and $7,391. For our example (you not seeking employment after retiring from the military), 90% of the first $1,226 equals $1,103.40. Calculating the benefit for the remainder of our average monthly earnings we multiply the amount over $1,226 by 32% ($3,158 minus $1,226 = $1,932): $1,932 x 32% = $618.24. Adding the two amounts together we get a full pension amount of $1,721.64, or $20,659 a year.

Working after you retire from the Military. If you continue working after you retire from the military, working 11 years and just earning the same as your E-7 basic pay, your 35-year average earnings for Social Security would jump from $37,900 a year to $61,427 a year ($5,119 a month); this would increase your Social Security pension by more than one third.

If we assume you just take a job making $10 an hour at a fast-food restaurant after retiring from the military (and never get a pay increase) you would earn $20,800 a year in Years 25 through 35. This additional (essentially minimum wage) income would increase your average monthly earnings for Social Security to $3,703. This increases your Social Security pension to $1,896 a month, or $22,752 a year. This is more than $2,000 a year above what you would get from Social Security if you stopped working when you retired after 24 years in the military.

If you continue working after the military (and most of you will), it is more likely that you will take a job earning about the same amount you were making in the military. If you continue earning $74,858 through Year 35, this additional income would increase your average monthly earnings for Social Security to $5,119 a month. Your Social Security pension would be $2,349 a month, or $28,188 a year. Assuming you draw Social Security retirement from the age of 67 until you die at the age of 85 (18 years), you would get an additional $135,522 in lifetime Social Security benefits from working the additional 11 years. This eliminates all "zero income" years from the Social Security calculation – and the benefit is significant – but this still has you stopping all paid employment after 35 years (at age 53). If you were to keep working, your higher income years after retiring from the military would begin to replace lower income years from the early part of your military career. If you were to work to full retirement age (67 years of age) at the same salary as your final basic pay in the military, you could replace your first 14 years of (relatively low) earnings with 14 high earnings years. In this case, your average monthly earning (for your highest paid 35 years; 10 in the military and 25 post-military) would be $6,128 and your Social Security pension at age 67 would be $2,672 a month (or $32,064 a year).

Because the model in this book assumes you get married, we will also assume that your spouse will receive a Social Security pension. For ease of calculations, we will assume that your spouse is your same age, and that both of you claim Social Security at your "Full Retirement Age" (67 years old). We will also assume that your spouse's lifetime income (highest 35 years) is less than yours. The model in this book assumed your spouse only worked during the first year of your marriage (until children entered the family). If your spouse's income is less than yours, they will be paid their full Social Security benefit plus an amount that brings their pension to an amount equal to half of yours. What this means is that if your spouse never worked paid employment, they would still receive a Social Security pension equal to half of yours when you both begin receiving Social Security benefits at age 67. In the example where you retire after 24 years in the military and never work again, your Social Security Pension was estimated to be 1,721.64 a month, or

$20,659 a year. In this case, your spouse's Social Security pension would be $860.82 a month, or $10,326 a year. Together your benefits total $30,985 a year. In the example where you continue working until the age of 67, your Social Security Pension was estimated to be $2,672 a month ($32,064 a year). In this case, your spouse's Social Security pension would be $1,336 a month, or $16,032 a year; your combined benefits would total $48,096 a year. The 25 years that you worked after retiring from the military will add $17,138 to your total income during retirement. Over the course of an 18-year retirement, this will be more than $300,000 in additional income.

The final factor that you must consider in planning your Social Security pension is the age at which you will start to draw that pension. You probably know that your "full retirement age" is 67 years. You can begin receiving benefits as early as the age of 62, but they will be reduced by 5/9 of 1% for each month before full retirement age, up to 36 months; after that, the reduction is 5/12 of 1% per month. In short, if you begin taking your Social Security pension at 62, you will only get 70% of the full pension you would have received at the age of 67. Conversely, if you delay taking your pension until after the age of 67, your benefit will increase by 8% for each year that you delay taking your pension (up to the age of 70). Obviously claiming your benefit early means you will get more checks during your life, but they will be smaller. Delaying your benefit will mean your checks are larger, but you will get fewer of them before you die. Many people have different opinions on the optimal age to begin taking Social Security, and there is no one "right answer" for everyone. I would suggest that the actuaries at the Social Security Administration are good enough at predicting your life span that the increases or decreases to your pension will largely be offset by the additional months you do, or do not, receive a check. I would think first about your spousal benefit. Because the model in this book assumes your spouse is not receiving a paycheck for most of their adult life, they are likely to draw a Social Security spousal benefit (a pension based on your earnings), rather than a pension based on their earnings.

If you claim your Social Security benefit early, this will also reduce your spouse's Social Security benefit, regardless of when they claim their pension. If you draw your Social Security before full-retirement age (67), your spouse will receive a reduced benefit. There is, however, no advantage to your spouse if you delay claiming your benefit until after full-retirement age.

VA Disability

The discussion of post-military employment should convince you that a "second career" after the military has a lot of benefits; hence, this is the path most military retirees choose. It is a fact, however, that serving in the military can be physically demanding and can expose you to environmental hazards that your non-military peers do not have to contend with. To compensate veterans for the hazards that can be involved in military life, the U.S. government requires the Veterans Administration (VA) to pay monthly compensation to veterans who are injured or sick due to their military service.

Of course, you would ideally complete your career without any negative health impacts. Fortunately, the statistics suggest this will be the case. As of 2021, fewer than 1 in 5 veterans leave the military with a condition that would justify the payment of disability compensation.[70]

Because the focus of this book, and the model it recommends, is focused on a career in the military, your risk of illness or injury will be higher than that of veterans who serve a single term in the military. If you do find that your health has suffered because of your military career, you can file a claim with the VA for compensation. Importantly, compensation payments from the VA are not subject to income tax.

In general, you cannot receive both a military retirement and VA disability compensation. For most retirees with a disability that entitles them to compensation from the VA, this means that they must waive a portion of their military retired pay to receive the VA disability compensation. The practical effect is that a disability essentially makes a portion of your retired pay tax-free. For example: Susan retires after 20 years and is entitled to $2,300 a month in military retired pay. She also has a disability rating of 20%, which entitles her to monthly compensation from the VA of about $325 a month. Assuming she is in the 12% tax bracket, she would owe about $250 a month in income tax on her retiree pay. Because the VA compensation is tax free, she would waive $325 of her military retirement and receive only $1,975 in military retired pay; this would allow her to receive the $325 in disability compensation from the VA. Although it seems she is still only receiving $2,300 a month ($1,975 military retirement and $325 VA disability compensation), her total income has actually gone up because she now owes only $237 (rather than $250) in income tax every month because her taxable retired income has been reduced. In effect, her 20% disability rating adds $13 a month to her spendable income.

For more severely disabled veterans, Congress has passed legislation that allows the concurrent receipt of military retired pay and VA disability compensation. If your service-connected disabilities are rated at 50% or higher, you can receive the full amount of your military pension and the full amount of your VA disability compensation. In the case of Susan (from the previous paragraph), if her disability rating were increased to 70%, she would not need to waive any of her military retired pay ($2300 a month) to receive the full $1,663 in VA disability compensation. With a severe disability (or disabilities) that result in a 70% disability rating (or higher), Susan is unlikely to be fully employed; this means she will not be like the servicemember in our example (in the discussion of post-military employment) who keeps earning $68,000 a year after they retire. Because the "healthy" veteran discussed above will earn almost a million dollars after retirement (a total of $953,000 earned after military retirement and before their "true retirement" at the age of 67) and will also earn a higher Social Security pension based on those additional earnings, the government tries to level the field by providing the severely disabled veterans with relatively substantial (and tax free) compensation.

The compensation paid to veterans with substantial disability ratings is not like "winning the lottery." As stated above, the severely disabled veterans may not be able to engage in post-military employment. Even if they can work, their disability will likely limit the work they can do and/or the amount of time they can engage in that work. Consider again that a totally disabled veteran is going to lose the ability to gain the $1,000,000 (perhaps more) in post-military income that their healthy counterparts are earning. Their Social Security pension will also be reduced because of this. Using the examples in the Social Security examples above our severely disabled veteran will receive a Social Security pension of $1,563 a month (potentially combining with their spouse's benefit for a monthly total of $2,345). Our healthy veteran, with higher lifetime earnings, will receive $2,430 from Social Security ($3,545 a month when the spouse's benefit is included). Both veterans will receive the same military retiree pension until they die at the age of 80, but the post-military earnings of the healthy veteran will total more than $1,506,000 ($953,000 from post-military employment and $553,000 from Social Security). The severely disabled veteran will receive just over $758,000 in disability compensation from the VA ($1,663 a month for 38 years) and $365,800 from Social Security, for a total of $1,124,000. In this case our healthy veteran reaches the end of their life with almost $400,000 more lifetime income and a lot less pain/inconvenience/frustration than the disabled veteran. Did our disabled veteran really "win the lottery"?

In 2025 disability benefits from the Veterans' Administration are shown below. The amounts shown reflect payments for a veteran with a spouse, but no children under the age of 18. In some cases, payments can be higher if you also have dependent children (or parents):

- 10% disabled $175.51 a month
- 20% disabled $346.95 a month
- 30% disabled $601.42 a month
- 40% disabled $859.16 a month
- 50% disabled $1,208.04 a month
- 60% disabled $1,523.93 a month
- 70% disabled $1908.19 a month
- 80% disabled $2,214.89 a month
- 90% disabled $2,489.96 a month
- 100% disabled $4,044.91 a month

As you have likely assumed, the higher the rating, the more sever the disability. That is absolutely correct. A 10% disability rating might be assigned for a condition that might be considered more "inconvenient" than "disabling." Conversely, a 100% disability rating means the veteran is totally disabled, and likely unable to work.

A veteran's overall disability rating is based on all conditions related to their military service. In other words, if the veteran has several disabling conditions, they will receive a combined rating that accounts for all their conditions. You might be tempted to think that you might finish your career with a total of ten conditions that each merit a 10% disability rating; add them together and you are 100% disabled. That is not the case. Some veterans refer to the VA system for determining combined disability ratings as "VA math," because it doesn't add up like normal math. You might think that a veteran with three conditions, each rated as 10% disabling, would receive a combined rating of 30%. And indeed, their combined rating would be 30%. You might now think that a veteran with three conditions rated as 40% disabling, 20% disabling, and

10% disabling, would receive a combined disability rating of 70% from the VA. Not so. This veteran would merit a combined disability rating of just 56% (which would be rounded up to 60%). The "VA math" used to determine combined ratings, begins with the highest rating (in the example above 40%). If we subtract that 40%, we are left with a veteran that is 60% healthy. We then take the second highest rating (20% in this case) and find that 20% of the 60% of the veteran that was "healthy" after subtracting the first rating equals a 12% rating for the second disability. Hence a veteran with 40% and 20% disability rating would be 52% disabled (which would be rounded down for a combined rating of 50%). Adding in the third rating (10% in this example), we have a veteran that is 52% disabled and therefore only 48% "healthy." We multiply the 10% rating by the 48% of the veteran that was still "healthy" after the last disability, and we find this condition is 4.8% disabling (rounded up to 5%). Adding the 5% to the previous 52%, we now give our veteran a combined disability rating of 57%, which would be rounded up to 60%. Let's return to the rhetorical question about the veteran with ten separate conditions, each rated as 10% disabling to see how "VA math" plays out for someone with many disabilities:

	Combined Rating	**Percent "Healthy"**
Condition 1:	**10%**	(100% - 10%) = 90%
Condition 2:	10% + (90% x 10) = **19%**	(100% - 19%) = 81%
Condition 3:	19% + (81% x 10) = **27%**	(100% - 27%) = 73%
Condition 4:	27% + (73% x 10) = **34%**	(100% - 34%) = 66%
Condition 5:	34% + (66% x 10) = **41%**	(100% - 41%) = 59%
Condition 6:	41% + (59% x 10) = **47%**	(100% - 47%) = 53%
Condition 7:	47% + (53% x 10) = **52%**	(100% - 52%) = 48%
Condition 8:	52% + (48% x 10) = **57%**	(100% - 57%) = 43%
Condition 9:	57% + (43% x 10) = **61%**	(100% - 61%) = 39%
Condition 10:	61% + (39% x 10) = **65%**	

You can see from this example that 10 x 10 does not equal 100. In "VA math," 10 x 10 equals a 65% rating (which rounds up to a 70% rating). Given the rounding that the VA does, a veteran with 11 or 12 conditions rated at 10% would also also get a combined rating of 70%. Veterans with 13, 14, 15, 16, or 17 conditions rated at 10% would all get an 80% combined rating. Indeed, a veteran with no disability rated higher than 10% would need a total of 27 disabilities rated at 10% to merit a combined rating of 100%.

CHAPTER 11

Considering Other Paths to Financial Independence

Because you are reading this book, I assume that you have enough financial wisdom to know there is no reliable way to "get rich quick." Of course, both of those terms ("rich" and "quick") are relative. This book will show you a reliable way to get rich, meaning achieving financial independence (you don't need to work if you don't want to). It will also show you how to achieve goal this relatively early in life (in your 40s and 50s, rather than working until you die).

There have always been people touting get-rich-quick schemes, and there always will be. We all want "more." And we want it "now." Someone will win the lottery; millions will not. Someone will develop a new technology that creates phenomenal wealth for them; billions will not. Someone will become a big musician, professional athlete, or movie star; millions will try and fail. The lure of getting rich quick is hard to resist. The odds of winning the lottery are about 1 in 300,000,000. That means that if you buy 10 tickets every week, it can still take more than 500,000 years (that is about as long as humans have been walking on two legs) for your numbers to come up. Statistically speaking, you are not going to win the lottery. But someone does win, and everyone focuses on the one person who did win, while ignoring the millions who lost. There are 1,696 active players in the NFL. That seems like a lot of people, but you need to consider that there are more than 1,000,000 kids playing high school football today. Of these, fewer than 20,000 will play the top tier of college football. Less than 80,000 of them will be lucky enough to play Division I football. Of those who do play Division I football, only about 250 will sign an NFL contract.[71] To put that into perspective, imagine everyone in Kansas City, Kansas playing high school football (and dreaming of an NFL career). Everyone in the entire town. Young and old. Plumbers, teachers, surgeons, retirees, infants; all wanting that NFL contract. The number of them that will ever actually play in the NFL would leave a school bus half-empty. Does it happen? Yes. Is it likely to happen? No.

One plan often proposed to help people build wealth quickly is real estate investing. Like the lottery and the NFL, some people do get wealthy with real estate; most do not. If you watch TV or peruse social media, you have almost certainly seen someone promoting real estate as the pathway to real wealth. Investing in real estate can work, but don't be fooled about two realities: 1) making money in real estate *is not quick*, and 2) making money in real estate *is hard work*. I've owned and managed single-family and multi-family rental units. Did I make money? Yes. A little bit. Did it take work? Yes. A lot.

Being a landlord is a job. Remember, financial independence means not having a boss (unless you want one). Financial independence means "If I don't want to get out of bed today, I'm not going to." When your tenant calls about a broken pipe at 3 O'clock in the morning, you will need to get out of bed. The rental unit is your boss; it tells you when you can and cannot take a day off – often with no warning. You may be telling yourself " I will just hire a property manager to answer those calls." You can absolutely do that, and many people do. But you need to know that hiring a property manager will eat up most (perhaps all) of your profit. People who have never owned rental properties have an impression that their landlord is sitting in his castle –wearing a black cape and top hat– plotting how he can heartlessly extract more money from his tenants. The reality is that the rental market is, of course, market driven. Being a landlord is also unlikely to lead to financial independence in less than several decades (when your mortgages are paid off).

Let's consider a hypothetical, but realistic, rental scenario. We are in an area where people can buy a house for $250,000. Let's say our potential landlord makes a 20% down payment ($50,000) and finances the remaining $200,000 of the purchase with a mortgage. We estimate their monthly costs (mortgage payment, insurance, and taxes –or "PITI" for Principle, Interest, Taxes and Insurance) to be $2,500. If this person then rents the house for $3,000 a month and hires a property manager (who takes 10% of the rent, $300, each month), the landlord's gross rental income is $3,000 each month, but their expenses are $2,800 each month. They are actually making a small net profit of $200 every month, and that not bad. However, fully understanding the wisdom of this investment requires us to consider four factors: Opportunity Cost, Vacancies, Maintenance, and Market Competition.

Opportunity Cost. Opportunity cost is economic term for potentially missing opportunities because you have your money committed to something else. In this scenario, our landlord has $50,000 of his money tied up (his down payment); leaving her unable to use that money for anything else. As a straightforward example of a "missed opportunity," we can just use the stock market as an alternative. Over the last 100 years, the Stock Market –using the Standard and Poor's 500 (S&P500) as our measure–has grown by just over 10% each year. If our landlord had not purchased the property, but invested the money in the stock market, we can assume she would make about 10% per year. That means that investing in the stock market would increase her wealth by about $5,000 per year on average, whereas the rental property is returning $2,400 per year –less than half of what she would be making if she just invested the down payment. More money and less hassle. There is indeed a "cost" involved in choosing to commit your money to buying rental properties.

Vacancies. Every rental property will be vacant for some period of time. If we assume that our landlord has priced her rental property such that it is always in demand, we'll assume that it is never vacant for more than one month when one tenant leaves and another moves in.

we will assume that our tenants rent on a one-year lease, and that the tenants never break their lease. Given these somewhat optimistic conditions, our landlord will only have to cover one month of expenses out of pocket (without any rental income) for only one month in any year that they have a change of tenants. That means they will only have eleven months where they made the $200 net profit ($2,200 for the year), but they have to cover all the costs for the one month that the property is vacant. They will have to pay $2,500 in expenses for that one month the property is empty; this means their "profit" for the year is actually a negative number! Any year there is any vacancy, our landlord will have to pay $300 out of pocket to be a landlord. Being a landlord is costing you money rather than making you money!

Maintenance. In any home, there will always be something that needs to be fixed. This can range from something as simple as replacing a light bulb for a few dollars, to something as significant as replacing the roof or heating system. On average, homes in the United States require about 3% (newer homes) to 5% of their value (older homes) in annual maintenance.[72] For our example, we will budget 4% of the home's value for repairs and maintenance. Thus, we need to expect that our $250,000 home will require us to spend (or set aside for larger repairs in the future) a total of $10,000 per year. In our example, we are making a "profit" of $200/month or $2,400 per year, but after we budget for maintenance and repairs, we find that we are actually losing money again! We are actually losing $7,600 every year by being a landlord!

Market Competition. I am sure that, as you read about each of the preceding factors, you are telling yourself "I would just raise the rent!" Now you are starting to sound like the evil landlord trying to extract more and more money from your tenants. The reality is that you cannot simply choose how much you will charge your tenants; the market will determine how much you can charge. Let's return to our example and see what we can charge for rent.

To cover vacancies and maintenance in our example, you would need to add those costs to your $2,500/month for PITI. If we add $300/

year to cover vacancies and $7,600/year to cover maintenance and repairs, this will add about $660/month to the amount we charge for rent. Our tenant now has to pay us $3,660/month. Because increasing the rent will increase the amount we are charged by our property manager by another $66/month, we need to cover this expense by increasing the rent even more. We'll say that we are now going to charge our tenants $4,000 per month. This covers our PITI ($2,500), our maintenance expenses ($10,000/year, or $833/month), our vacancy costs ($2,500/year or $209/month), and our property management fees (now $400/month). Our expenses total $3,942/month, and our income is $4,000 per month. We now have a net profit of $58 per month. At this point, it is worth reflecting back on Opportunity Costs: "$58 a month return on my $50,000 investment! I could make more money by just putting my down payment in a savings account!" If we want our money (our $50,000 down payment) to return at least as much as the stock market average, we need to price our rental to ensure we make at least $5,000/year ($417/month) in net profit. Thus we need to add at least another $359 ($417 minus the $58 in profit our $4,000/month rent makes for us). This brings the amount we need to charge for rent to $4,360.

As our landlord offers her rental property for $4,360 per month –because she isn't greedy, she just wants to make at least as much as she could get from investing her money in the stock market– but she is soon hit with the reality that no one wants to rent the home she is offering. Why? Because she has priced herself out of the market. When we offered the home for $3,000/month we had plenty of potential tenants calling, but raising the rent by almost 50% has, unsurprisingly, caused our potential renters to look elsewhere. "Isn't everyone charging the same amount?" "Are the other landlords losing money?"

The reality here is that you have some landlords who are willing to answer the phone at 4am so that they don't have to pay a property manager $400 a month; they can rent the same property for $3,960 a month. You also have some landlords who willing to forego a property manager and are willing (and able) to do most of the maintenance themselves.

This will offset much –although not all– of the $833 we are budgeting for repairs and maintenance, allowing them reduce the rent by another $500/month to $3,460 a month. No wonder no one is looking at your property that you want to rent for $4,360 a month. Again, you don't determine how much rent you charge; the market determines what you can charge for rent. You could also choose to do all the work yourself. It can be a lot of work, and it does require a variety of skills (plumbing, electrical, etc.). This will reduce your expenses; allowing you to reduce what you charge for rent and thereby make your property more appealing to potential tenants. The reality here is that you have just taken on a second job. The worst part of your second job is that you don't get a paycheck; most of the financial benefit is just the fact that you have tenants in your property. If you choose to be the landlord who "does it all themselves" so that you can rent for $3,460 a month, your second job will only pay you $418 a month ($3,460 in rent minus $2,500 for PITI, $209 for vacancy allowance, and $333 for expenses (even doing all the work yourself, you still need to pay for supplies, equipment and some specialty tools).

Making $418 a month isn't bad. But considering all the work you are doing (answering the phone at 3 O'clock in the morning *AND* driving to your rental for *YOU* to fix the leaking toilet), your mind will quickly drift back to Opportunity Cost. You now remember that your money $50,000 down payment would probably be earning about $5,000 a year ($417/month) in net profit. You are doing all this work for a net gain of $1 a month over just investing in the stock market. That $1 a month is a lot less minimum wage. Is this really a job that you want?

Another factor in the market is the large-scale landlord. This is the person with many properties, who employs a plumber, electrician, etc. on an almost daily basis (one of the many properties will need something almost every day of the year). This ongoing relationship the tradespeople they employ allows them to get a sort of volume discount; significantly reducing their maintenance and repair expenses; the same applies to the fees their property manager charges them. They can charge a lower amount for rent without having to fix toilets themselves, but their income doesn't have to come from a single property; rather, they make a relatively small profit on each of their many properties that adds up to enough to make the venture worthwhile for them. They will be competing with you for tenants, and they will almost always be able to offer similar properties at lower prices, and likely with better service. In sum, being a landlord does not mean you are getting "free money." Being a landlord probably means work, a perhaps a lot of work. Being a landlord means your investment is probably earning less than you could have made in the stock market. Being a landlord definitely does not mean you will be getting rich quick.

Capital Appreciation. You may now be saying "I don't need to make a monthly profit on my rental property. I'll just have the rent cover my expenses and then sell the house thirty years from now for ten times what I paid for it!" The stories of your great uncle Steve who bought his house 90 years ago for 10 cents and sold it last year for $1,000,000 may be true, but what they ignore is that when Steve bought the house, 10 cents was equal to about 20 years pay; just as the $1,000,000 he sold it for is equal to about 20 years pay. The truth is great uncle Steve didn't really make a profit. You should know that over the *best* 30 years in the housing market, houses only appreciated by 2.2 percent per year, about the same as the rate of inflation. For the worst thirty years in the housing market, prices were actually 2 percent lower at the end of thirty years![73] The reality is this: relative to inflation, houses don't actually grow in value. Yes, there are periods of rapid price increase (and decrease), but in the long-term, housing prices essentially just keep pace with inflation. Real estate is not a reliable way to grow wealth. Most of the people who are getting rich from real estate are the ones selling other people on the idea that you can get rich in real estate.

CHAPTER 12

Conclusion

I hope you are reading this book as a forward-thinking 18-year-old. As someone in early adulthood, you have an incredible opportunity to develop genuine wealth. I therefore hope that reading this book has convinced you to take action to achieve financial independence. If you follow the plan laid out in this book you will become genuinely wealthy. You will have the discipline to "pay yourself first," funding your future before spending on unnecessary things.

You have learned that the military compensation package is much more than just basic pay. You have learned that military compensation is very generous indeed, so much so that you can enjoy the same lifestyle as the average non-military American family and still grow a pile of money that will support a comfortable retirement. You know that there is no reliable way to "get rich quick." But you have the knowledge necessary to chart a path through life that will result in you becoming wealthy at a relatively young age. Importantly, you have a clear road map to help you arrive at this enviable position without having to live a pauper's life while you are young. You are ready to take action to became wealthy while still enjoying the same standard of living as your peers outside the military.

During your career, you will probably also enjoy some of the added benefits that military service can entail. Living overseas is one great opportunity that you probably enjoyed. Many Americans visit other countries, but living overseas for several years can offer the sort of immersive experience that most American will never know. Your children will also benefit in other ways from being raised in a military family. Research has shown that children in military families have a higher median Intelligence Quotient (IQ) than their civilian counterparts.[74] Relatedly, the academic performance of children in military families exceeds the academic performance of their civilian peers.[75] Finally, children from military families are also more likely to have a college degree as adults than their civilian counterparts.[76] Your military career will help your children on their path through life even before the GI Bill helps to pay their college tuition.

Your spouse will enjoy many of the same aspects of a military career, although maintaining a career can be especially challenging for a military spouse due to the frequent moves. Nonetheless, you know that you can raise a family, enjoying the same quality of life as most American, and not require two incomes. The extra income a spouse could make, can be a benefit, but you now know it is not essential.

Importantly, you are equipped to embark on a military career with a solid understanding of your military compensation. You know that allowances of any kind– are not "free money" and that your BAS will not always appear in your paycheck (i.e., if the military is providing your meals). This knowledge will help you understand they "why" of many aspects of military compensation; avoiding the frustration experienced by your colleagues who are ignorant about how their pay and allowances work. You also understand the straight-forward program that will allow you to convert your military compensation. Summarized in just 16 steps across a 24-year military career:

- As an E-1, you begin by contributing 37% of your basic pay to the TSP.
- When you are promoted to E-2, you increase your TSP contributions to 45% of your basic pay.
- As an E-3, you will contribute 47% of your basic pay.
- Upon promotion to E-4, your contributions go to 51%
- Increase to 53% when going over three years of service.
- As an E-5, increase contributions to 56% of your basic pay
- You then decrease contributions to 44% when you turn 25
- Going over eight years of service, you increase to 46%.
- You decrease TSP contributions to 42% of your basic pay to provide you with the extra spending money needed to support your new spouse.
- When you go over ten years of service you will be able to increase TSP contributions slightly (to 43%)
- After the birth of your first child, you reduce contributions to 23%.
- Outside of the TSP, you invest 100% of your Continuation Pay in an IRA (between eight and twelve years of service).
- When you go over twelve years of service, you increase TSP contributions to 29%
- You increase contributions again (to 30% of your basic pay), when you go over fourteen years of service.
- Your final increase (to 35%) comes with promotion to E-7
- When you turn 35 years-old, you decrease your contributions to 5%, and leave them at that level for the rest of your career.

At the end of your military career, you will have earned a pension that will pay you a healthy amount for the rest of your life. As you progress through your post-military years, you will acquire additional streams of income. At the age of 59½, you will be able to withdraw funds from your TSP without penalty or taxes. You will also be able to draw on any funds you put into IRAs (either traditional or Roth), although you will have to pay income tax on money taken from a traditional IRA. Between the age of 62 and 70, based on your decision, you will also begin drawing a pension from Social Security. Collectively, these income streams will be more than adequate to ensure that you have ***a lifetime of income that is well above that of most Americans***. Americans over the age of 65 have an average income of about $5,361 a month.[77] The defined benefit portion of your military retirement will provide you with $2,959 every month. Social Security will provide you at least $1,721.64 (assuming you stop working at age 43). Your TSP account will provide the bulk of your retirement income ($5,750 a month, assuming a 4% rate of withdrawal beginning at age 59½). Together you will have a consistent income of $10,430 a month ($125,000 a year) for the rest of your life, almost twice as much as the average American. The journey you started 40 years ago is complete. You will have achieved financial independence! Congratulations.

ENDNOTES

CHAPTER ONE

[1] Costa, Dora L. "The Evolution of Retirement: An American Economic History, 1880-1990." *NBER*, 1 Jan. 1998, www.nber.org/books/cost98-1.

[2] Laskow, Sarah. 2014. "How Retirement Was Invented." *The Atlantic*. October 24, 2014. https://www.theatlantic.com/business/archive/2014/10/how-retirement-was-invented/381802/.

[3] O'Neill, Aaron. 2021. "United States: Life Expectancy 1860-2020." Statista. February 3, 2021. https://www.statista.com/statistics/1040079/life-expectancy-united-states-all-time/.

[4] U.S. Congress. United States Code: Social Security Act, 42 U.S.C. §§202- Suppl. 4 1934.

[5] U.S. Social Security Administration. "Social Security History." n.d. www.ssa.gov. https://www.ssa.gov/history/lifeexpect.html.

[6] U.S. Congress. United States Code: Social Security Act, 42 U.S.C. §§801- Suppl. 4 1934.

[7] "Social Security History." n.d. www.ssa.gov. https://www.ssa.gov/history/tftable.html.

[8] Steuerle, C. Eugene and Smith, Karen E. "*RESEARCH REPORT: Social Security and Medicare Benefits and Taxes: 2023.*" The Urban Institute. July 2023.

[9] "Number of Social Security Recipients by Type of Beneficiary." n.d. www.ssa.gov. https://www.ssa.gov/cgi-bin/currentpay.cgi

CHAPTER TWO

[10] "Barista Salary in New York State." 2025. Indeed.com. 2025. https://www.indeed.com/career/barista/salaries/New-York.

[11] "Fashion Writer Salary in New York City, NY." ZipRecruiter. February 12, 2025. https://www.ziprecruiter.com/Salaries/Fashion-Writer-Salary-in-New-York-City,NY.

[12] Loftey. "NYC Rent per Square Foot: Getting the Most Space for Your Money." *Loftey | NYC's #1 Apartment Locators*, 23 July 2024, loftey.com/nyc-rent-per-square-foot-getting-the-most-space-for-your-money.

[13] Bowers, Lois A. "One-fifth of Americans 59+ Have Net Worth of $0 or Less." *McKnight's Senior Living*, 25 Apr. 2024, www.mcknightsseniorliving.com/news/one-fifth-of-americans-59-have-net-worth-of-0-or-less.

[14] Bureau of Labor Statistics. "Median Usual Weekly Earnings of Full-Time Wage and Salary Workers by Age and Sex." n.d. Www.bls.gov. https://www.bls.gov/charts/usual-weekly-earnings/usual-weekly-earnings-current-quarter-by-age.htm.

[15] Bureau of Labor Statistics. "Table 9. Quartiles and Selected Deciles of Usual Weekly Earnings of Full-Time Wage and Salary Workers by Selected Characteristics, 2024 Annual Averages - 2024 Q05 Results." 2024. Bureau of Labor Statistics. 2024. https://www.bls.gov/news.release/wkyeng.t09.htm.

[16] Bureau of Labor Statistics. "Median Usual Weekly Earnings of Full-Time Wage and Salary Workers by Age and Sex." n.d. www.bls.gov. https://www.bls.gov/charts/usual-weekly-earnings/usual-weekly-earnings-current-quarter-by-age.htm.

[17] Bureau of Labor Statistics. "Median Usual Weekly Earnings of Full-Time Wage and Salary Workers by Age and Sex." n.d. www.bls.gov. https://www.bls.gov/charts/usual-weekly-earnings/usual-weekly-earnings-current-quarter-by-age.htm.

[18] "Tables." *Bureau of Labor Statistics*, 25 Sept. 2024, www.bls.gov/cex/tables.htm.

[19] "Tables." *Bureau of Labor Statistics*, 25 Sept. 2024, www.bls.gov/cex/tables.htm.

[20] "Tables." *Bureau of Labor Statistics*, 25 Sept. 2024, www.bls.gov/cex/tables.htm.

[21] "Tables." *Bureau of Labor Statistics*, 25 Sept. 2024, www.bls.gov/cex/tables.htm.

[22] Tice, Jim. 2015. "New Rules for Enlisted Promotions." Army Times. February 23, 2015. https://www.armytimes.com/news/your-army/2015/02/23/new-rules-for-enlisted-promotions/.

[23] Powers, Rod. n.d. "Simplified Form of Marine Corps Enlisted Promotion System." The Balance Careers. https://www.thebalancecareers.com/enlisted-promotions-made-simple-3332773.

[24] Bajza, Stephen. 2019. "Air Force Enlisted Ranks." Military.com. 2019. https://www.military.com/air-force/enlisted-ranks.html.

[25] "Killeen, TX Cost of Living." 2022. Bestplaces.net. 2022. https://www.bestplaces.net/cost_of_living/city/texas/killeen.

[26] "QuickFacts: Killeen City, Texas." 2024. Census Bureau QuickFacts. United States Census Bureau. 2024. https://www.census.gov/quickfacts/fact/table/killeencitytexas/POP060210.

CHAPTER THREE

[27] Bureau of Labor Statistics. BLS Report: "Consumer Expenditures in 2023." December 20, 2024. https://www.bls.gov/opub/reports/consumer-expenditures/2023/home.htm.

[28] "Life Insurance Rates by Age." n.d. Bankrate. https://www.bankrate.com/insurance/life-insurance/rates-by-age/#how-life-insurance-rates-are-determined.

[29] "Family Servicemembers' Group Life Insurance (FSGLI)." 2020. Veterans Affairs. September 17, 2020. https://www.va.gov/life-insurance/options-eligibility/fsgli/.

[30] "Rates : LiveOn." n.d. Liveon.psu.edu. https://liveon.psu.edu/rates.

[31] "Meal Plans : LiveOn." n.d. Liveon.psu.edu. https://liveon.psu.edu/altoona/meal-plans-old.

CHAPTER FOUR

[32] Bureau of Labor Statistics. "Median Usual Weekly Earnings of Full-Time Wage and Salary Workers by Age and Sex." n.d. www.bls.gov. https://www.bls.gov/charts/usual-weekly-earnings/usual-weekly-earnings-current-quarter-by-age.htm; Bureau of Labor Statistics. "Consumer Expenditures Survey (CEX)." April 26, 2018. https://www.bls.gov/cex/tables.htm.

[33] Bureau of Labor Statistics. "Median Usual Weekly Earnings of Full-Time Wage and Salary Workers by Age and Sex." n.d. www.bls.gov. https://www.bls.gov/charts/usual-weekly-earnings/usual-weekly-earnings-current-quarter-by-age.htm.; Bureau of Labor Statistics. "Consumer Expenditures Survey (CEX)." April 26, 2018. https://www.bls.gov/cex/tables.htm.

[34] Guzman, Gloria, and Melissa Kollar. 2024. "Income in the United States: 2023." Census.gov. United States Census Bureau. September 10, 2024. https://www.census.gov/library/publications/2024/demo/p60-282.html.

[35] Bureau of Labor Statistics. BLS Report: "Consumer Expenditures in 2023." December 20, 2024. https://www.bls.gov/opub/reports/consumer-expenditures/2023/home.htm.

[36] Threewitt, Cherise. 2020. "Car Depreciation: What Factors Affect Car Values?" US News & World Report. U.S. News & World Report. 2020. https://cars.usnews.com/cars-trucks/advice/car-depreciation-what-factors-affect-car-values

[37] Parekh, Nishant and Campau, Todd. "Average Age of Vehicles Hits New Record in 2024." 2024. IHS Markit. May 22, 2024. https://www.spglobal.com/mobility/en/research-analysis/average-age-vehicles-united-states-2024.html.

[38] Kopp, Daniel. 2021. "How Much Is Your Military Pay Really Worth?" The Military Wallet. September 8, 2021. https://themilitarywallet.com/much-military-pay-worth/.

CHAPTER FIVE

[39] US Census Bureau. 1967. Consumer Income: Income in 1965 of Families and Persons in the United States. January 12, 1967. https://www2.census.gov/prod2/popscan/p60-051.pdf

[40] Mitchell, Cory. 2022. "Average Historical Stock Market Returns for S&P 500 (5-Year up to 150-Year Averages)." Trade That Swing. August 9, 2022. https://tradethatswing.com/average-historical-stock-market-returns-for-sp-500-5-year-up-to-150-year-averages/.

[41] "Is Inflation High Compared to Years Past? Breaking down Inflation Rates by Year." Forbes. January 2, 2023. https://www.forbes.com/sites/qai/2023/01/02/is-inflation-high-compared-to-years-past-breaking-down-inflation-rates-by-year/?sh=1d7238746d7a.

[42] Kent, Ana Hernandez, and Lowell Ricketts. 2020. "Wealth Inequality in America over Time: Key Statistics | St. Louis Fed." www.stlouisfed.org. Federal Reserve Bank

of St. Louis. December 2, 2020. https://www.stlouisfed.org/open-vault/2020/december/has-wealth-inequality-changed-over-time-key-statistics.

[43] "News and Insights." 2021. Nasdaq.com. 2021. https://www.nasdaq.com/articles/whats-your-net-worth-25-of-americans-say-theirs-is-$0-or-less.

CHAPTER SIX

[44] United States Census Bureau. 2023. "Figure MS-2 Median Age at First Marriage: 1890 to Present." https://www.census.gov/content/dam/Census/library/visualizations/time-series/demo/families-and-households/ms-2.pdf.

[45] Workman, Simon. 2021. "The True Cost of High-Quality Child Care across the United States." Center for American Progress. June 28, 2021. https://www.americanprogress.org/article/true-cost-high-quality-child-care-across-united-states/.

[46] Bureau of Labor Statistics. 2024, "CONSUMER EXPENDITURES – 2023." September 25, 2024. https://www.bls.gov/news.release/pdf/cesan.pdf

[47] Westrick-Payne, Krista K. "Median Age at First Marriage: Geographic Variation, 2022." 2022. Bowling Green State University. 2022. https://www.bgsu.edu/ncfmr/resources/data/family-profiles/median-age-first-marriage-geographic-variation-2022-fp-24-08.html.

CHAPTER SEVEN

[49] Bureau of Labor Statistics. "Median Usual Weekly Earnings of Full-Time Wage and Salary Workers by Age and Sex." n.d. www.bls.gov. https://www.bls.gov/charts/usual-weekly-earnings/usual-weekly-earnings-current-quarter-by-age.htm.

[50] "Tables." *Bureau of Labor Statistics*, 25 Sept. 2024, www.bls.gov/cex/tables.htm.

[51] "Tables." *Bureau of Labor Statistics*, 25 Sept. 2024, www.bls.gov/cex/tables.htm.

CHAPTER EIGHT

[52] "Tables." *Bureau of Labor Statistics*, 25 Sept. 2024, www.bls.gov/cex/tables.htm.

CHAPTER NINE

[53] Westrick-Payne, Krista K. "Median Age at First Marriage: Geographic Variation, 2022." 2022. Bowling Green State University. 2022. https://www.bgsu.edu/ncfmr/resources/data/family-profiles/median-age-first-marriage-geographic-variation-2022-fp-24-08.html

[54] "Tables." *Bureau of Labor Statistics*, 25 Sept. 2024, www.bls.gov/cex/tables.htm.

[55] U.S. Bureau of Labor Statistics. "Usual Weekly Earnings of Wage and Salary Workers: Fourth Quarter 2024." *U.S. Bureau of Labor Statistics*, report, USDL-25-0072, 22 Jan. 2025, www.bls.gov/cps.

[56] "Tables." *Bureau of Labor Statistics*, 25 Sept. 2024, www.bls.gov/cex/tables.htm.

[58] "Tables." *Bureau of Labor Statistics*, 25 Sept. 2024, www.bls.gov/cex/tables.htm.

[59] Workman, Simon. 2021. "The True Cost of High-Quality Child Care across the United States." Center for American Progress. June 28, 2021. https://www.americanprogress.org/article/true-cost-high-quality-child-care-across-united-states/.

[60] Statista Research Department. 2018. "Average Number of Own Children per Family U.S. | Statista." Statista. Statista. 2018. https://www.statista.com/statistics/718084/average-number-of-own-children-per-family/.

[61] "Tables." *Bureau of Labor Statistics*, 25 Sept. 2024, www.bls.gov/cex/tables.htm.

[62] "Tables." *Bureau of Labor Statistics*, 25 Sept. 2024, www.bls.gov/cex/tables.htm.

[63] U.S. Bureau of Labor Statistics. "Usual Weekly Earnings of Wage and Salary Workers: Fourth Quarter 2024." *U.S. Bureau of Labor Statistics*, report, USDL-25-0072, 22 Jan. 2025, www.bls.gov/cps.

[64] "Tables." *Bureau of Labor Statistics*, 25 Sept. 2024, www.bls.gov/cex/tables.htm.

CHAPTER TEN

[66] https://tricare.mil/-/media/Files/TRICARE/Publications/FactSheets/Costs_Fees.pdf

[67] "Veteran and Civilian Pay." 2024. Hill & Ponton, P.A. May 21, 2024. https://www.hillandponton.com/resources/veteran-and-civilian-pay-statistics/.

[68] See, for example, "What Is the 4% Rule for Retirement | New York Life." n.d. Www.newyorklife.com. https://www.newyorklife.com/articles/four-percent-rule-retirement.

[69] Zialdo, Katie. "What Is the Average Mortgage Payment?" n.d. www.rocketmortgage.com. https://www.rocketmortgage.com/learn/average-mortgage-payment.

[70] US Census Bureau. 2021. "Census Bureau Releases New Report on Veterans." Census.gov. November 10, 2021. https://www.census.gov/newsroom/press-releases/2021/veterans-report.html.

CHAPTER ELEVEN

[71] "Odds of High School Players Going pro: Football and Concussions." n.d. u.osu.edu. https://u.osu.edu/groupbetaengr2367/junran-add-things-here-for-real/.

[72] Wolf, Josh. 2022. "The Truth about the Annual Cost of Home Maintenance - HomeKeep™." HomeKeep™. January 25, 2022. https://homekeep.com/learning-center/the-truth-about-the-annual-cost-of-home-maintenance.

[73] Bilello, Charlie. 2023. "How to Think about Home Price Appreciation." Creative Planning. March 23, 2023. https://creativeplanning.com/insights/investment/home-price-appreciation/.

CHAPTER TWELVE

[74] Kenny, James A. "The Child in the Military Community." *Journal of the American Academy of Child Psychiatry*, vol. 6, no. 1, Jan. 1967, pp. 51–63. https://doi.org/10.1016/s0002-7138(09)61289-9.

[75] Esqueda, Monica Christina, et al. "A Call to Duty." *Educational Researcher*, vol. 41, no. 2, Mar. 2012, pp. 65–70. https://doi.org/10.3102/0013189x11432139..

[76] Williams, K.C. and L.L. Mariglia, "Military Brats: Issues and Associations in Adulthood." *Military Brats and Other Global Nomads: Growing up in Organization Families*, edited by Morten Ender, Praeger, 2002, pp. 67-82.

[77] Bureau of Labor Statistics, *Consumer Expenditures in 2023,* 20 Dec. 2024, www.bls.gov/opub/reports/consumer-expenditures/2023/home.htm.

www.ingramcontent.com/pod-product-compliance
Lightning Source LLC
LaVergne TN
LVHW022055200926
848481LV00003B/915
* 9 7 9 8 3 4 9 2 1 4 8 8 2 *